Kabbalah, Astrology, and Tarot for Beginners

Unlocking Ancient Jewish Mysticism, the Zodiac Signs, Natal Chart Reading, Divination, Numerology, and Psychic Development

Your Free Gift
(only available for a limited time)

Thanks for getting this book! If you want to learn more about various spirituality topics, then join Mari Silva's community and get a free guided meditation MP3 for awakening your third eye. This guided meditation mp3 is designed to open and strengthen ones third eye so you can experience a higher state of consciousness. Simply visit the link below the image to get started.

https://spiritualityspot.com/meditation

Or, Scan the QR code!

Table of Contents

Part 1: Kabbalistic Astrology

The Ultimate Guide to Hebrew Astrology for Beginners, Ancient Jewish Mysticism, Zodiac Signs, Interpreting Your Kabbalah Natal Chart, and Qabalistic Tarot Reading

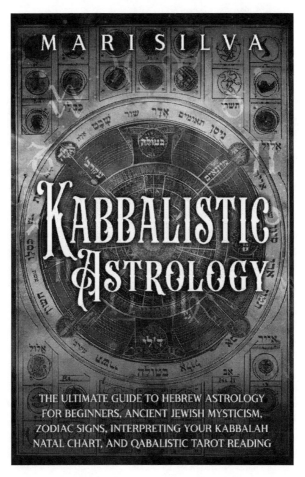

Introduction

Religion, in some form, has existed for thousands of years. While the specific doctrines, core values, and expressions of each religion vary, they all share the belief in something beyond the material world. Although some religions put their faith in relatively simple concepts easily understood by any layperson, some religions choose to delve deeper into the mysteries surrounding the universe. Many traditional religions have offshoots studying mysticism and esotericism, dealing with the spiritual and metaphysical energy they believe exists just beyond the perceivable world.

When a group of people gets together to explore arcane and occult knowledge, they tend to be pushed to the fringes of society. Because of this, secret fraternities, brotherhoods, and organizations are often established to give those interested in these types of subjects a safe place to practice sacred rituals and share their ideas. Some of these "secret" societies are no longer hidden from plain view. The Freemasons, for example, have been plastered on the forefront of popular culture for years now, to the point where the very idea that Freemasonry could be harboring any sort of hidden agenda these days is laughable.

The Illuminati, based on the very real organization known as the Bavarian Illuminati, which was forcibly disbanded by 1787, has become a catchall for secret societies supposedly operating in the shadows. In reality, while there have been some poor attempts at resurrecting the Illuminati, they primarily exist within the realms of fiction in the form of convenient antagonists who behave cryptically and leave enigmatic clues all over for the heroes to decipher, ultimately thwarting an ill-defined plot for power. The fact remains that secret organizations from history only hid from public view because they existed during a time when any deviation from popular ideas, discourse, and religious practices could result in a death sentence for those who were caught. It was a mechanism purely driven by survival – not world domination.

Nowadays, most forms of religion or their offshoots can be practiced freely without fear of imprisonment or execution. This doesn't mean people won't ostracize or disparage someone for doing it. Still, outside of the areas where religion is strictly mandated and regulated by the state, there is little danger in publicly revealing your belief system. Things like paganism, Wicca, new age spirituality, esotericism, and mysticism have gained a significant following since the turn of the 21st century. Technology and communications have evolved to the point where it isn't very difficult to find like-minded individuals who share your interests. This is especially true for non-traditional religions and religious practices.

One of the more popular religious systems in the world today is Kabbalah. It saw exponential growth after a collection of high-profile celebrities began practicing it. However, there is a lot more to Kabbalah than someone may share on social media or talk about in red-carpet interviews. It has roots stretching back to ancient Judaism. Astrology is another form of esotericism with a prevalence in modern society. Suppose you've ever read your horoscope or looked into your zodiac sign. In that case, you will have at least a passing familiarity with it. Both Kabbalah and Astrology deeply connect to the spiritual and metaphysical side of the universe. While there are plenty of mysteries yet to uncover, learning more about them can help shine a light on some very interesting aspects of your life that you may never have known before. Anyone fascinated by the idea that you can discover your inner spirit or receive portends of the future is sure to love reading this book and learning more about it.

Chapter 1: When Kabbalah Meets Astrology

Kabbalah and astrology are both important pillars of Western esotericism. There is a rich history behind Kabbalah and its development from its inception to the modern day. Astrology has an even longer tradition among many different cultures, from ancient China, Babylon, India, Mesopotamia, and the Mayan Empire. There is a significant amount of crossover between the two practices. Astrology has an important place within Kabbalah regarding reading natal charts, studying zodiac signs, and interpreting Tarot cards. There is plenty to learn about Kabbalah and astrology and how they intermingle to comprehensively examine your personality, characteristics, ambitions, and past, present, and future.

Kabbalah has a rich history with its connection to astrology.
https://pxhere.com/en/photo/848342

What Is Kabbalah?

Kabbalah is an ancient Jewish tradition of mysticism that seeks to uncover the mysteries of God and the universe. The central teachings of Kabbalah include the concept of the Ein Sof, a divine being beyond human comprehension, and the idea that the universe is a manifestation of the Ein Sof's emanations, known as sephirot. Kabbalah strongly emphasizes studying the Zorah, or Hebrew Bible, and other sacred texts. Meditation, rituals, and prayer are used as a means to connect with the divine and gain a deeper understanding of the hidden aspects of the universe. The ultimate goal is to achieve spiritual enlightenment and a better understanding and awareness of the self.

History of Kabbalah

The history of Kabbalah can be traced back to 12th-century Spain and Southern France, particularly the region of Provence, where Jewish mystics and scholars began to explore a new understanding of Jewish theology and spirituality. These early Kabbalists drew upon earlier Jewish mystical traditions such as Merkabah and Hekhalot mysticism. They were also influenced by Neoplatonism and Gnosticism, as well as the writings of the French rabbi Isaac the Blind. Kabbalah has substantially impacted various other religious and philosophical movements, including Hasidic Judaism, Hermeticism, Christian Cabala, and Hermetic Qabalah.

A significant milestone in Kabbalah's history was the publication of the Zohar in the 13th century by Spanish rabbi and mystic Moses de León. This book is considered the foundation of Kabbalistic literature. It contains interpretations of scripture, noting instances of mysticism in the Torah, as well as content concerning mythical psychology and mythical cosmogony. It also delves into spiritual and philosophical concepts, such as God's nature, the universe's creation and structure, the essence of souls, the path to redemption, the relationship between the ego and darkness, the "true self," and the Light of God.

Kabbalah was originally a restricted work and not widely taught to the general populace of the Jewish world. However, this began to change after a series of hardships endured by the Jewish community during the Middle Ages, with the rise of antisemitism. This culminated with the Alhambra Decree (Edict of Expulsion), a joint edict issued by Isabella I of Castile and Ferdinand II of Aragon, the Catholic monarchs of Spain, which ordered all practicing Jews to vacate their kingdoms and territories in 1492. This act aimed to hamper the Jewish people's growing religious and economic influence. There was a fear that if they controlled the banks and loans, it would erode the power of the Crown. Isabella and Ferdinand also worried that many of Spain's recently-converted "New Christian" population would revert back to Judaism, diminishing the prestige and control of the Catholic Church.

Antisemitism continued to spread throughout the 16th century. As a result of the shared cultural trauma the Jewish people suffered, there was an increase in the belief that the arrival of a "Jewish Messiah" was imminent. The Jewish Messiah was entirely separate from the Christian Messiah or Jesus Christ. Still, their function in their respective religions was very similar. The Jewish populace held out hope that their Messiah would come and save them, delivering them from exile and redeeming the faithful. This form of messianism was encouraged by Jewish mystics from Safed, a small settlement in the region of Galilee, which now forms part of northern Israel.

There was a struggle for prominence within Kabbalism between the doctrine laid out in the Zohar and the tenets of the Safed mystics. The teachings of Isaac Luria, a leading rabbi and mystic from Safed, sparked the biggest transformation in Kabbalah, which adopted many of his messianic beliefs. Lurianic Kabbalism reinterpreted the Idra, which was the most esoteric section of the Zohar. It emphasized the beliefs of reincarnation, messianism, and "Tohu and Tikkun." Tohu and Tikkun depict the nature of duality, with Tohu meaning chaos and confusion, while Tikkun represents order and rectification. Luria's teachings are considered equally fundamental to Kabbalah as the Zohar.

The widespread acceptance of Kabbalah within Jewish culture saw it gain more influence on the people. In 1540, it was decided that the fundamentals of Kabbalah must be taught publicly to people of all ages. According to the Jewish mystics, only when Kabbalah had spread to the four corners of the world would violence, hatred, destruction, and war come to an end, allowing peace, harmony, and love to reign in the days leading up to the coming of the Jewish Messiah. Once this happened, time and space would shrink, while the people would learn the secrets of immortality.

Kabbalah had a major impact on the development of Hasidism. This spiritual movement endorsed the immanence of God, which taught that he was present throughout the universe. It also promoted the idea that one should strive to maintain a personal relationship with Him at all times, as well as the importance of devotion in religious practices and the spiritual significance of physical actions and daily life. In Hasidic Judaism, adherents are divided into "courts" or "dynasties," each one led by a Rebbe, who serves as their spiritual leader.

In the first half of the 18th century, "modern" Kabbalah started to take form. The Italian rabbi and philosopher Moshe Chaim Luzzatto established a "yeshiva," or a Jewish educational institution that focuses on halacha (Jewish law) and the Talmud, for the specific purpose of giving students a place to study Kabbalah. Although Luzzatto was eventually forced to close his yeshiva and turn over his writings on the subjects of Kabbalah and mysticism, his works which managed to survive, are often a starting point for people who wish to immerse themselves in the esoteric side of Judaism.

Kabbalah also significantly influenced the development of mysticism in other religions, such as Christian Cabala and Hermetic Qabalah. Christian Cabala emerged in the 16th century and adapted the beliefs of Kabbalah to Christian theology. It mainly developed among Christian scholars who studied Jewish kabbalistic texts as they sought to prove the truth of Christianity through the lens of mysticism and esoterica. Christian Cabala also emphasizes the spiritual significance of the Bible and Christian liturgy.

Hermetic Qabalah, also known as Hermeticism, emerged as a form of mysticism in the late medieval period. It is based on a syncretic blend of Kabbalah, Christian Cabala, Neoplatonism, Gnosticism, and several other spiritual and philosophical traditions. Hermetic Qabalah is often associated with the Hermetic Corpus, a group of texts from the Hellenistic period that taught Hermeticism principles. It emphasizes the study of the Tree of Life, a mystical symbol representing the path to enlightenment and the microcosm and macrocosm relationship.

At the turn of the 21st century, Kabbalah was thrust into the limelight due to several famous celebrities revealing themselves as Kabbalists. This included Madonna, Ashton Kutcher, and his then-wife, Demi Moore, Britney Spears, Gwyneth Paltrow, Paris Hilton, and Lindsay Lohan. However, many of them gave it up by the mid-2010s, as they weren't willing to devote themselves completely to religion. Instead, celebrities and those they influenced viewed Kabbalah as a shortcut to spiritual enlightenment, wielding its core tenets as a self-help weapon. Despite the celebrities and influencers losing interest in it, Kabbalah continues to be studied and practiced by many Jews and non-Jews alike. It is considered one of the most important spiritual traditions in Jewish history.

What Is Astrology?

Astrology is a belief system that holds that the positions and movements of celestial bodies, like the sun, moon, and planets, influence human behavior and the natural world. It is thought that the locations of celestial bodies at the time of a person's birth can predict certain characteristics and life events and explain aspects of their personality, relationships, and omens for the future. With its roots in ancient cultures, particularly in the Near East and the Mediterranean, astrology survives and is still widely practiced.

Astrology is the belief system that interprets the stars' effects on our lives.
ESA/Hubble, CC BY 4.0 <https://creativecommons.org/licenses/by/4.0>, via Wikimedia Commons https://commons.wikimedia.org/wiki/File:Starsinthesky.jpg

The core idea of astrology is that the universe is ordered and that the movements of the celestial bodies reflect patterns and cycles which can be understood, interpreted, and predicted. It is divided into several branches, including natal astrology, concerned with studying an individual's birth chart, and mundane astrology, which focuses on studying astrological influences on world events and large groups of people. Learning how to read charts, stars, and alignments is the first step to becoming an astrologist. It isn't always easy, but it can be incredibly rewarding once you figure it out.

It is important to note that astrology is not the same thing as astronomy, which is the study of celestial objects and phenomena that originate outside the Earth's atmosphere. Astrology isn't considered a hard scientific discipline but a pseudoscience and type of divination. Where astronomy is purely focused on what can be observed or inferred by the laws of nature, astrology deals more with psychology, emotions, and behavior. It can be difficult to definitively prove the veracity of astrology. Still, those who take it seriously and try to do it right are often pleasantly surprised by the positive results.

History of Astrology

Astrology originates in many disparate ancient civilizations, including the Mayans, Chinese, Indians, Babylonians, Egyptians, and Greeks. The Babylonians are credited with developing the first system of astrology around 2,400 BCE, which they used primarily for predicting eclipses and other celestial events. The first text to describe astrology appeared around 1,400 BCE in the Indian subcontinent and was called the Vedanga Jyotisha. The Mayans had their own form of astrology, using the stars to determine different signs and track the passage of time on their infamous calendar. The Mayan year was only 260 days, divided into 13 galactic numbers (similar to months), with 20 days in each galactic number.

In ancient Egypt, astrology was closely tied to religious beliefs and was used to predict the fate of the pharaohs and the kingdom. The Egyptians also developed a form of horoscopic astrology, which uses the position of the sun, moon, and planets at the time of a person's birth to make predictions about their future. The ancient Greek version of astrology was influenced by the works of philosophers such as Pythagoras and Plato, who believed in the connection between the celestial realm and the human world. The Greek system of astrology was later adopted by the Romans, who spread it throughout their empire.

Astrology was widely accepted as a legitimate discipline in Europe during the Middle Ages. Monarchs often used it to make decisions about state affairs. It also played a role in the development of modern astronomy, as many early astronomers were also astrologers. However, during the scientific revolution of the 16th and 17th centuries, astrology lost ground as a science, as it was found to be unable to provide reliable predictions, which many wrote off as akin to superstition. Today astrology is mainly used for self-help, entertainment, and self-exploration.

Kabbalah, Astrology, and Western Esotericism

Kabbalah, astrology, and western esotericism are all forms of spiritual and mystical thought seeking to explore hidden knowledge, understand the influence of celestial bodies, and aim for spiritual enlightenment. While the three share some commonalities and can be practiced together, each has its own specific teachings and traditions with distinct differences. Kabbalah is more focused on God and the universe, especially with the prominence of sacred texts documenting the history of the Jewish people. Astrology is primarily concerned with the movements of celestial bodies, their positions relative to one another, and how these can influence human affairs and the natural world. Western esotericism encompasses a broad range of mystical and spiritual traditions and experienced its development within Western societies, including practices like Rosicrucianism, hermeticism, alchemy, and theosophy.

Kabbalistic Calendar

The Kabbalistic calendar is a unique calendar that's separate from the Gregorian calendar. It's based on the cycle of lunar months, and as with all calendars centered on the moon's phases, there are times when it will lag behind, necessitating the addition of temporary months. Because this calendar was specifically designed for Kabbalah, it allows individuals to align their spiritual practices, rituals, and mystical beliefs with the universe's energies. According to Kabbalah, certain days and times are more conducive to specific aspects of these customs, so its calendar lets individuals identify those days and times.

The Kabbalah calendar is divided into four phases that correspond to the four worlds of Kabbalah: Atzilut, Beriah, Yetzirah, and Asiyah. Each phase is connected to a different stage in the spiritual journey and is associated with distinctive spiritual practices. It is divided into 72 weeks, with each week correlated with a specific sephirah, or attribute, of God. Each week is associated with a certain custom or meditation, assisting in their spiritual alignment. It's important to note that the Kabbalah calendar is not widely used by traditional Jewish communities and is considered part of modern Kabbalah scholarship, as opposed to the original interpretation. Although the traditional Jewish calendar is also based on lunar cycles, the calendar specifically tied to Kabbalah is rejected by many leaders within Judaism.

How the Kabbalistic Calendar Works

The days in the Kabbalistic calendar are each considered positive, negative, or neutral days. Positive days possess abundant energy and are ideal for starting new projects like getting married, purchasing a new home, planting seeds in a garden, or embarking on a new business venture. The days particularly strong with positive energy are the first days of each month, which coincide with the new moons. Starting the month by taking advantage of the first day's positive energy can extend that energy to the entire month.

Negative days lack energy, which makes them the opposite of positive days. Things in your life initiated on negative days have a greater chance of failure since the entire venture will be imbued with negative energy. Neutral days don't have more or less energy, remaining entirely balanced between the two sides. You can start a venture on a neutral day and still see success, but it will be more difficult than if you did so on a positive day. Conversely, your chances of experiencing failure will be less than if you started it on a negative day.

The Jewish Holy Day, known as Shabbat, begins at sundown every Friday and ends at sunset on Saturday. Kabbalists believe that Shabbat is the only day of the week when the spiritual and physical realms align, boosting the amount of positive energy during this period. The flow of spiritual energy is also heightened during Shabbat, making it available for personal connections and individual growth. Shabbat allows practitioners to access a higher level of their souls and change their destinies for the upcoming week.

Holidays celebrated during the Jewish year are not just about tradition. They are imbued with a lot of positive energy, making them powerful tools for personal growth and improvement. These holidays serve as cosmic portals in time that allow for connection to various frequencies of positive spiritual energy, which can help eliminate negativity and chaos, leading to increased fulfillment in life. Each holiday offers a unique channel to access this spiritual energy and learn how to grow as a person.

Months of the Kabbalistic Calendar

- **Nisan:** This is the 1st month by the ecclesiastical reckoning and the 7th month (8th during leap years) by the civil reckoning of the Kabbalistic calendar. Nisan contains 30 days. It is roughly the equivalent of March to April in the Gregorian calendar. Major Jewish holidays which fall within Nisan include Passover and Akitu.

- **Iyar:** This is the 2nd month by the ecclesiastical reckoning and the 8th month (9th during leap years) by the civil reckoning of the Kabbalistic calendar. Iyar contains 29 days. It is roughly the equivalent of April to May in the Gregorian calendar. Pesach Sheni and Lag Baomer are celebrated during this month.

- **Sivan:** This is the 3rd month by the ecclesiastical reckoning and the 9th month (10th during leap years) by the civil reckoning of the Kabbalistic calendar. Sivan contains 30 days. It is roughly the equivalent of May to June in the Gregorian calendar. The Jewish holiday of Shavuot is celebrated within Sivan.

- **Tammuz:** This is the 4th month by the ecclesiastical reckoning and the 10th month (11th during leap years) by the civil reckoning of the Kabbalistic calendar. Tammuz contains 29 days. It is roughly the equivalent of June to July in the Gregorian calendar. The fast day known as the Seventeenth of Tammuz falls within this month.

- **Av:** This is the 5th month by the ecclesiastical reckoning and the 11th month (12th during leap years) by the civil reckoning of the Kabbalistic calendar. Av contains 30 days. It is roughly the equivalent of July to August in the Gregorian calendar. The Jewish holidays of Tisha B'Av and Tu B'Av are celebrated during Av.

- **Elul:** This is the 6th month by the ecclesiastical reckoning and the 12th month (13th during leap years) by the civil reckoning of the Kabbalistic calendar. Elul contains 29 days. It is roughly the equivalent of August to September in the Gregorian calendar. Elul is traditionally a month of repentance undertaken in preparation for the High Holy Days during Tishrei.

- **Tishrei:** This is the 7th month by the ecclesiastical reckoning and the 1st month by the civil reckoning of the Kabbalistic calendar. Tishrei contains 30 days. It is roughly the equivalent of September to October in the Gregorian calendar. In addition to celebrating the Jewish New Year, major Jewish holidays falling within Tishrei include the High Holy Days of Rosh Hashanah and Yom Kippur.

- **Cheshvan:** This is the 8th month by the ecclesiastical reckoning and the 2nd month by the civil reckoning of the Kabbalistic calendar. Cheshvan contains 29 or 30 days, depending on whether or not Rosh Hashanah is postponed that year. It is roughly the equivalent of October to November in the Gregorian calendar. Marcheshvan and the Fast of Behav fall within Cheshvan.

- **Kislev:** This is the 9th month by the ecclesiastical reckoning and the 3rd month by the civil reckoning of the Kabbalistic calendar. Kislev contains 29 or 30 days, depending on whether or not Rosh Hashanah is postponed that year. It is roughly the equivalent of November to December in the Gregorian calendar. The major Jewish holiday of Hanukkah falls within Kislev.

- **Tevet:** This is the 10th month by the ecclesiastical reckoning and the 4th month by the civil reckoning of the Kabbalistic calendar. Tevet contains 29 days. It is roughly the equivalent of December to January in the Gregorian calendar. If Kislev is short, Hanukkah will end in Tevet. The fast day known as the Tenth of Tevet also falls within this month.

- **Shevat:** This is the 11th month by the ecclesiastical reckoning and the 5th month by the civil reckoning of the Kabbalistic calendar. Shevat contains 30 days. It is roughly the equivalent of January to February in the Gregorian calendar. Tu Bishvat, a Jewish holiday celebrating the renewal of the trees, falls within Shevat.

- **Adar:** This is the 12th month by the ecclesiastical reckoning and the 6th month by the civil reckoning of the Kabbalistic calendar. Adar contains 29 days. It is roughly the equivalent of February to March in the Gregorian calendar. During leap years, Shevat is followed by Adar Aleph or Adar I, a 30-day intercalary month. Adar Aleph is then followed by this month, called Adar Bet or Adar II. Major Jewish holidays that fall within this month include Purim, the Feast of Esther, and the fast day known as the Seventh of Adar, which honors the death of Moses.

Kabbalistic vs. Gregorian Calendars

Although there are some crossovers and similarities between the Kabbalistic and Gregorian calendars, some key differences set them apart.

The Gregorian calendar is based on solar cycles for establishing the months and years, while the Kabbalistic calendar is lunar-based. Most of the principal calendars worldwide are lunar calendars, with only the Julian and Gregorian calendars using solar years. The Gregorian calendar is the primary one used in Western civilizations, so it is often the calendar with which most people in the West are familiar. It makes no attempt to synchronize with the moon's cycles, despite the prevalence of lunar-based calendars throughout the rest of the world.

The Gregorian calendar is synchronized with one full revolution around the sun, which takes approximately 365.2422 days. Most years possess 365 days, with months containing either 30 or 31 days, except for February, which has 28. To account for the extra fraction of a day and realign the calendar year with the Earth's revolution around the sun, a "leap day" is added to the end of February every 4 years, known as "leap years." However, the calendar will still be slightly off after a century or so. To remedy this, every year exactly divisible by 100 will not be a leap year, but centurial years that can be divided by 400 *exactly* will be leap years. This means the years 1700, 1800, and 1900 were not leap years, but 2000 was a leap year.

Meanwhile, the Kabbalistic calendar will almost always have a new month that coincides with a new moon and lasts until the end of the lunar cycle. The Kabbalistic calendar will sometimes add a 13th month to a particular year to account for the discrepancies built up over several years due to the months synching to the lunar cycle instead of the solar cycle. This normally occurs every 2 to 3 years over a 19-year cycle, with seven leap years during the cycle. The additional month is placed between Shevat and Adar, the 11th and 12th months, respectively, by the ecclesiastical reckoning. It essentially splits Adar into two months, the first containing 30 days and the second having the usual 29 days.

The extra months are marked by an epithet of the first two letters from the Hebrew alphabet, "Aleph" and "Bet," or simply by adding the Roman numerals of "I" and "II" to the end of Adar. Part of the reason for synching the Kabbalistic calendar with the solar calendar is to ensure that the Jewish holidays also remain synchronized with the Gregorian calendar. This makes it easier for those who practice Kabbalah and Judaism in general while living in the Western world to celebrate their major holidays at approximately the same time every year.

The leap years of the Kabbalistic calendar are determined by the Metonic cycle, which is based on the fact that there are roughly 235 lunar months in 19 solar years. The years 3, 6, 8, 11, 14, 17, and 19 within the 19-year cycle are leap years. To determine whether a Kabbalistic year is a leap year, find its position within the 19-year Metonic cycle. This position is calculated by dividing the Kabbalistic year number by 19 and finding the remainder. For example, if the Kabbalistic year 5782 (the equivalent of the year 2022 CE in the Gregorian calendar) is divided by 19, it results in a remainder of 6, indicating that it is a leap year. Note that there is no year 0 in the Jewish calendar, so a remainder of 0 means that the year is the 19th of the Metonic cycle, which is a leap year.

Another difference from the Gregorian calendar is that the Kabbalistic calendar can add or subtract days to prevent major Jewish holidays like Rosh Hashana from falling on certain days of the week. A day can be added to Cheshvan, the 8th month, or it can be subtracted from Kislev, the 9th month. Ultimately, these adjustments result in any given year in the Kabbalistic calendar can have 6 different lengths. Common years can have 353, 354, or 355, while leap years can have 383, 384, or 385 days. Years with 353 or 383 days are known as deficient years; years with 354 or 384 are known as regular years; and years with 355 or 385 days are known as complete years.

Kabbalistic and Astrological Principles

Kabbalistic astrology uses chart readings – just like in other forms of astrology – to aid in self-discovery, realizing your potential, and improving your ability to communicate and express your ideas, visions, and emotions. It can also help you understand how to interact effectively with others. Each person is born with unique talents and challenges associated with their astrological sign. These signs serve as guides, highlighting problems that must be overcome and identifying your purpose in life. The ultimate goal of kabbalistic astrology is to transcend the effects of the universe and assert control over your own life.

The Zodiac signs do not determine your personality traits so much as your personality dictates your sign. The karma acquired in a previous life determines which sign you need to be born under to gain the attributes and characteristics necessary to correct past mistakes, find personal growth, and improve yourself into a better version of yourself. Ideally, you will eventually reach the point where you have become your best self, which means you can find oneness with God. This is a critical point to the teachings of Kabbalah, especially as it was laid out by the patriarch Abraham around 3,800 years ago in the text called Sefer Yetzirah, the Book of Formation. Abraham is considered Kabbalah's very first astrologist.

The biggest difference between Kabbalistic astrology and other forms of astrology is that the former uses a lunar calendar, and the latter tends to use solar calendars, particularly the Gregorian calendar. While the names for the Zodiac in Kabbalah remain the same, each sign corresponds to a single Kabbalistic month rather than being split across two months like it is with the Gregorian calendar. The Kabbalastic months and their Zodiac signs are as follows:

- **Aries (Nisan):** The Ram (Hebrew Name: Taleh)
- **Taurus (Iyar):** The Bull (Hebrew Name: Shor)
- **Gemini (Sivan):** The Twins (Hebrew Name: Teomim)
- **Cancer (Tammuz):** The Crab (Hebrew Name: Sartan)
- **Leo (Av):** The Lion (Hebrew Name: Aryeh)
- **Virgo (Elul):** The Virgin (Hebrew Name: Betulah)
- **Libra (Tishrei):** The Scales (Hebrew Name: Moznaim)
- **Scorpio (Cheshvan):** The Scorpion (Hebrew Name: 'Aḳrav)
- **Sagittarius (Kislev):** The Archer (Hebrew Name: Ḳashat)
- **Capricorn (Tevet):** The Goat (Hebrew Name: G'di)
- **Aquarius (Shevat):** The Water-Bearer (Hebrew Name: D'li)
- **Pisces (Adar I and Adar II):** The Fish (Hebrew Name: Dagim)

The Role of Kabbalistic Astrology in Tarot Reading

Kabbalistic astrology plays an important role in Tarot reading, providing a framework for interpreting the meanings and symbolism of Tarot cards. Kabbalah, as an ancient Jewish mystical tradition, focuses on the spiritual aspects of the universe and the connection between God, humanity, and the world. Since it teaches that everything in the universe is interconnected, Tarot cards can be used to understand and access the hidden wisdom of the universe. It provides a spiritual and mystical perspective on the Tarot deck and helps uncover the hidden wisdom and insights the Tarot cards can offer.

In Tarot reading, the approach using Kabbalistic astrology offers an understanding of how the Tree of Life, a major Kabbalistic symbol, relates to the universe's structure. The Tree of Life consists of ten sephirot, or emanations, which correspond to the major arcana cards of the Tarot. The sephirot represent different aspects of the universe and the human experience, which can be used to understand the deeper meanings of the Tarot cards. Kabbalah also teaches the concept of the "Ein Sof," God's infinite and unknowable aspect. This connects to the "Unknowable" cards in Tarot, like the High Priestess and the Hermit.

Chapter 2: The Kabbalistic Tree of Life

The Kabbalistic Tree of Life is well-known for its mystical powers and insight. It has long been a part of the traditions of Kabbalah, stemming back to professor and philosopher Paolo Riccio's 1516 CE Latin translation of Gates of Light, written by Spanish Kabbalist Joseph Gikatilla. The earliest modern incarnation of the Kabbalistic Tree of Life was designed by the German scholar Johann Reuchlin, although this version lacked the full array of possible paths between the spheres. Reuchlin's design appeared on the cover of Gates of Light; later, Kabbalists would increase the original 17 paths within the Tree of Life to 21 or 22 paths. In the late 1600s, German Kabbalist Christian Knorr von Rosenroth wrote and published Kabbala Denudat, in which he introduced an updated version of the Tree of Life that had 11 spheres to complement the 22 paths for the first time.

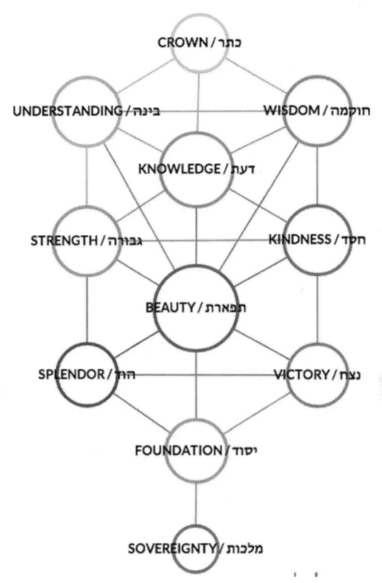

CROWN / כתר

UNDERSTANDING / בינה ——————— WISDOM / חוקמה

KNOWLEDGE / דעת

STRENGTH / גבורה ——————— KINDNESS / חסד

BEAUTY / תפארת

SPLENDOR / הוד ——————— VICTORY / נצח

FOUNDATION / יסוד

SOVEREIGNTY / מלכות

A simplified version of the Kabbalistic Tree of Life.
*Ideasfisherman, CC BY-SA 3.0 <https://creativecommons.org/licenses/by-sa/3.0>, via Wikimedia
Commons https://commons.wikimedia.org/wiki/File:Kabbalahtree.png*

Additional updates of the diagram continued throughout the 18th and 19th centuries, but there were still several distinct versions that placed the individual nodes in different positions. Part of this was due to the discovery of new planets in the solar system. Originally, most of the Tree of Life designs only contained Mercury through Uranus. Still, after Neptune and Pluto were confirmed to exist, these were included in updated versions while preserving the 22 paths of older designs. By the 21st century, the Kabbalistic Tree of Life had a relatively consistent design used by most sources. When Pluto was downgraded from a planet to a dwarf planet in August 2006, this, fortunately, did not affect the Tree of Life since the most commonly used design already positioned it as a "hidden sphere," so nothing needed to be changed to accommodate its adjusted status.

What Is the Tree of Life?

The Kabbalistic Tree of Life is a mystical diagram of interconnected nodes based on the traditional Jewish Tree of Life that serves as a major symbol within Kabbalah. It represents the structure of the universe and the path to enlightenment, offering multiple possible avenues to achieve them. The Tree comprises ten spheres, or sephirot, which are connected by 22 paths. Each sephirah represents a different aspect of God and the universe, and the paths between them symbolize the soul's journey to enlightenment. The tree is also seen as a map of the soul itself and the quest of the individual's attempt to connect with the divine.

The Tree of Life visually represents the universe's superior and inferior dimensions. It illustrates the concept that everything outside of us also exists within us, and the Tree of Life is a prime example of a macrocosm existing within a microcosm. It guides people to awaken their higher consciousness and return to where they originated, illustrating the microcosm. The Tree also represents the potential for humanity to do the same, which would be the macrocosm. The Tree of Life is derived from the manifestations known as the Ain, the Limitless, and the Absolute. The flow of celestial forces into the act of creation is what shapes and forms each sephirah. Just as water will spill from one tier of a fountain to the next, each sephiroth becomes denser than the one which came before it and has more rules and boundaries.

Role in the Macrocosm

In the Kabbalistic Tree of Life, the macrocosm is the overall result of every sephiroth and path working in unison toward a shared goal. Just as each sphere is an individual piece of a larger puzzle, every person who has ever lived was created in the image of God, but they lack the knowledge and power of God. Only when a person transcends their individualistic nature and rejoins God as a part of the whole do they become a fully-realized piece of the divine. This is also depicted in how the individual planets comprise the solar system. Zooming out farther, the planets of our solar system revolve around the sun, which is merely one star in a galaxy filled with stars. Taking it one more step beyond, our galaxy is one of *many galaxies* across the known universe.

Role in the Microcosm

The microcosm in the Kabbalistic Tree of Life is represented by the individual sephirah, with each one possessing certain characteristics and traits that feed into the Tree as a whole. The sephirot ultimately work together, connected by the 22 paths, to achieve the shared goal of harmonic relations to Creation and the universe. Each planet has its own environment and ecosystems, but the only one teeming with life is the Earth. All the people and their cities, towns, countries, and continents make up the whole of the Earth and serve as a microcosm of the larger universe. Zooming in more, you can view each individual as possessing their own microcosm of a universe within themselves, especially regarding the vast and uncharted seas of the mind, body, and soul.

Connection to Sacred Geometry

Sacred geometry is the belief that there are geometric shapes and proportions which can be assigned divine meaning. These sacred shapes and proportions prove that God is the Creator of the universe since it would be impossible for a purely random and self-perpetuating universe to possess these types of designs. Many mathematical forms can be observed in nature, either through their geometric patterns or behaviors. Because of this, the Kabbalist viewpoint is that it must have been created deliberately, and the Creator must be God. These beliefs are borne out in the structure and purpose of the Tree of Life.

Sacred geometry is shapes that are assigned divine meanings.
Violetcabra, CC0, via Wikimedia Commons
https://commons.wikimedia.org/wiki/File:Sacred_Geometry_Construction_with_Color.jpg

The Four Worlds of Kabbalah

The Four Worlds of Kabbalah are the realms of spiritual essence and emanation, including a descending chain of Existence. They are named Atziluth, Beriah, Yetzirah, and Assiah. Each realm with the Four Worlds design sits at a different level and has its own functions within the Kabbalistic cosmology. The Four Worlds are believed to have been imbued with the creative life force of Ein Sof, also called the Divine Creator or God. However, the Four Worlds don't only refer to their position within the universe or their role in its creation – they can also represent the levels of consciousness that exist in the human psyche or experience.

Atziluth

Atziluth is the first and highest realm of the Four Worlds. Other names for it include the World of Emanations or the World of Causes. It manifests within the top three sephirot in the Tree of Life. The realm of Atziluth is considered eternal, representing pure divinity, and is connected to the emanation of God's essence, or the free act of the will of God. The sephirot of Atziluth are an expression of the closeness of this realm in proximity to the Creator. All of creation is considered to spring from this realm, originating everything that has been, is, or ever will be. It is identified with the element of fire.

Beriah

Beriah is the second realm of the Four Worlds, the next one down from Atziluth. The other name for it is the World of Creation. It is associated with the sephirot of wisdom and understanding. Beriah works in conjunction with the realm above it, as it is where the ideas and concepts of Atziluth are given their form and tangible expression. This is the realm of the divine intellect and is purported to be the source of the archangels and spiritual realms. Beriah is also considered the realm of pure thought, where the sephirot remain in their purest form but are now being used to create and sustain the universe. Unlike Atziluth, which is eternal and made by the emanation of God, Beriah was created with a definitive point of origin. It is identified with the element of air.

Yetzirah

Yetzirah is the third realm of the Four Worlds and sits below Beriah. The other name for it is the World of Formation. It is associated with the middle sephirot of the Tree of Life, representing love, kindness, and justice. This is where the ideas and concepts of Beriah are given their shape and structure. The realm is split into two halves: "half good" and "half evil." The half-good manifests as emotional sensitivity and the desire to make others happy, while the half-evil is seen as a being's self-consciousness and negative emotions. It gave the creations of God a more concrete form and helped to organize the layout of the universe. Yetzirah is where the lesser angels and stars originate, as well as the place where the souls of human beings can interact with the spiritual world and seek passage to the higher realms. It is identified with the element of water.

Assiah

Assiah is the fourth and lowest realm of the Four Worlds. The other name for it is the World of Action. This is where the ideas and concepts coalesced within Yetzirah and are given solid form and manifestation. It is the source of the material world and the physical universe. Assiah is associated with the sephirot of power and foundation, where the attributes of God are completely hidden, and His creations have become entirely independent from Him. Human beings dwell here and interact with the physical world, where their ultimate goal is to immerse themselves in spiritual practice to elevate their souls from Assiah to the higher realms.

The Seven Chakras

The word "chakra" translates to "wheel," referring to areas on your body that contain a significant amount of complex points of spiritual energy. They are likened to disks of energy constantly spinning and needing to remain open and aligned. Chakras are an ancient system that first developed in India around 1500 to 1000 BCE. Their first mention came in the Vedas, a collection of sacred texts of spiritual learning written during this same period of antiquity.

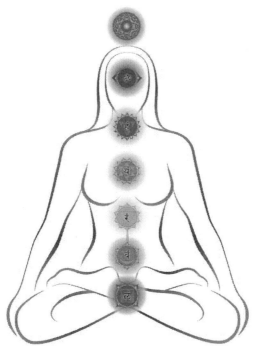

Each chakra corresponds to major organs and nerves that affect your spiritual and physical well-being.

Each chakra point corresponds to collections of nerves and major organs around your body that influence your physical, emotional, and spiritual health. While there are as many as 114 different chakras, the seven primary chakras run along your spine and have the greatest effect on you. Each individual chakra can resonate with people at different times. Certain chakras may be a continuous source of blockages for some, while these blockages may be temporary for others. In the chakra system, these patterns have specific terms and recommended treatments. The seven primary chakras each have a name, number, color, and specific location along your spine that is connected to them.

Root Chakra

Number: 1

Kabbalistic Name: Yesod

Area: Base of the spine

Represents: Personality, balance, and tradition

Color: Red

The root chakra, or *Muladhara* in Sanskrit, is the first of the seven chakras. It is located at the base of the spine and represents the foundation of your being, being closely linked to your survival instincts, physical identity, and grounding to the earth. You will feel safe, stable, and secure when your root chakra is open and balanced. You'll also feel a sense of belonging and connectedness to your physical body and the world around you. On the other hand, when your root chakra is blocked or imbalanced, you might feel listless, anxious, or disconnected from your physical body. Symptoms of a blocked root chakra include fatigue, muscle pain, and lower back pain.

Sacral Chakra

Number: 2

Kabbalistic Name: Hod-Nezah

Area: Below the belly button

Represents: Satisfaction, creativity, and pleasure

Color: Orange

The sacral chakra, also known as *Svadhishthana* in Sanskrit, is the second of the seven chakras. It is located in the lower abdomen, just below the navel, and represents your emotional and creative energy. This chakra is also associated with the feeling of pleasure and romantic pursuits. When the sacral chakra is open and balanced, you will feel emotionally stable and open to new experiences. You may feel a sense of creativity and healthy romantic energy. If the sacral chakra is blocked or imbalanced, you can become emotionally unstable, have difficulty with boundaries, or possess a low libido. Symptoms of an imbalanced sacral chakra may include lower back pain, hip pain, and romantic dysfunction.

Solar Plexus Chakra

Number: 3

Kabbalistic Name: Tiferet

Area: Upper abdomen

Represents: Confidence and self-worth

Color: Yellow

The solar plexus chakra, also known as Manipura in Sanskrit, is the third of the seven chakras. It is located in the abdomen, above the navel. This chakra has a strong association with the element of fire. The solar plexus chakra governs your personal power, will, and self-esteem. When it is open and balanced, you will be more confident, possess a sense of purpose, have more self-control, and maintain a positive self-image. A blocked or imbalanced solar plexus chakra can manifest as feelings of powerlessness, a lack of self-worth, and difficulty when making important decisions. Blockages can cause digestive issues, including heartburn, indigestion, ulcers, and eating disorders.

Heart Chakra

Number: 4

Kabbalistic Name: Gevurah-Hesed

Area: Center of the chest

Represents: Love, empathy, and mercy

Color: Green

The heart chakra, also known as Anahata in Sanskrit, is the fourth of the seven chakras. It is located in the center of the chest, directly above the heart. This chakra governs emotions such as love, compassion, mercy, and self-acceptance. An open and balanced heart chakra allows you to connect with others, feeling a strong sense of affection, appreciation, and acceptance. When it is blocked or imbalanced, you could experience physical or emotional issues related to your heart and circulatory system. It can also affect your relationships, creating difficulties between you and others and harming your emotional well-being. Some practices used to balance the heart chakra include meditation, yoga, and energy healing.

Throat Chakra

Number: 5

Kabbalistic Name: Da'at

Area: The throat

Represents: Communication and instruction

Color: Blue

The throat chakra, also known as Vishuddhi in Sanskrit, is the fifth of the seven chakras. It is located within your throat and the surrounding area. This chakra controls your ability to communicate and impart knowledge to others. It governs your thyroid gland, vocal cords, mouth, and ears. When the throat chakra is open and balanced, you will have an easier time verbalizing your point of view, making your feelings clear, and listening with compassion and understanding. Your confidence will shine through because you can speak your truth. When it is blocked or imbalanced, you might find it difficult to express yourself or feel heard, and you are less likely to listen or comprehend what others are trying to tell you. Physical symptoms of a blocked throat chakra include health issues such as a sore throat or thyroid issues.

Third Eye Chakra

Number: 6

Kabbalistic Name: Binah-Hokhmah

Area: Between the eyes on the forehead

Represents: Perception, innate knowledge, and imagination

Color: Indigo

The third eye chakra, also known as Ajna in Sanskrit, is the sixth of the seven chakras. It is located in the center of the forehead, between the eyebrows, and is often depicted as a purple or indigo lotus flower with two petals. This chakra is associated with intuition, wisdom, and spiritual insight. It governs your pituitary gland, pineal gland, eyes, and brain. When the third eye chakra is open and balanced, you will have a strong intuition, the ability to think clearly, and a deep sense of inner knowing. When it is blocked or imbalanced, it can manifest as confusion, lack of direction, and difficulty in making decisions. Physical symptoms due to a blockage include headaches, sinus issues, or eye problems.

Crown Chakra

Number: 7

Kabbalistic Name: Keter

Area: Top of the head

Represents: Consciousness and mental acumen

Color: White or violet

The crown chakra, also known as Sahasrara in Sanskrit, is the seventh of the seven chakras. It is located at the very top of your head and has a connection to all the other chakras and their corresponding organs in your body, including your brain and nervous system. This chakra represents the connection of your physical form to your spiritual purpose and enlightenment. When your crown chakra is open and balanced, it can help keep all the other chakras open, bringing you a sense of inner peace and spiritual fulfillment. However, if this chakra is blocked or imbalanced, you may appear to be closed-minded, skeptical, or inflexible.

The Sephirot

Sephirot (singular: sephirah) are defined as emanations through which Ein Sof and the infinite are revealed. They are constantly creating the physical realm and the higher metaphysical realms of the Four Worlds. The sephirot are arranged in multiple levels within the Tree of Life, representing where their corresponding realms are positioned within the hierarchy of the universe. There are ten regular sephirot within the Tree of Life and one elevated sephirah, organized in a descending chain from heaven to earth, like the Four Worlds. Their names and numbers are: 0-Kether, 1-Chokmah, 2-Binah, 3-Da'at, 4-Chesed, 5-Geburah, 6-Tiferet, 7-Netsach, 8-Hod, 9-Yesod, and 10-Malkuth.

The Tree of Life and the Seven Chakras

0. Keter is the highest of the sephirot, also known as *Crown*, and is positioned above all the others. It is labeled as

"superconsciousness" and is an eternal state of being an infinite source of creation. There is no limit to the potential of what is conceived and produced here, as well as producing a never-ending number of possibilities. It is the ultimate metaphysical reality, represented by the color gold. This sephirah denotes purification, flexibility, and conductivity.

1. Chochmah is part of the Intellectual Triad or Supernal Triangle found beneath Keter and is also known as Wisdom. It is the sephirah of insight, intuition, inspiration, unformed awareness, and a germinating idea. Chochmah embodies the emergence of something from nothing, represented by the color navy blue.

2. Binah is part of the Intellectual Triad or Supernal Triangle, also known as Understanding. It is the sephirah that expresses the expansion of an idea, the plotting of a story, and the establishment of the structure. Binah depicts the formation of concepts and matter, represented by the color dark red.

3. Da'at is part of the Intellectual Triad or Supernal Triangle and is also known as Knowing. It is the sephirah showing the identification and integration of ideas, creating an intimate connection between them and the divine. Da'at depicts the naming and application of that which is creation, represented by the color gray.

4. Chesed is part of the Emotional Triad and Ethical Triangle, found beneath the Intellectual Triad, and is also known as Unbounded Love. The sephirah expands ideas, widens their sphere of influence, and expresses empathy. Chesed depicts personal growth and concern for others, represented by the color blue.

5. Geburah is part of the Emotional Triad or Ethical Triangle, also known as Strength of Boundaries. It is the sephirah that encourages the setting of limits, communicating refusal, and looking for focus. Geburah depicts the establishment of strong boundaries, represented by the color red.

6. Tiferet is part of the Emotional Triad or Ethical Triangle, also known as Beauty. It is the sephirah that synchronizes opposing energies and shows compassion to others. Tiferet depicts harmony and kindness, represented by the color yellow.

7. Netsach is part of the Instinctual Triad and Magical Triangle, found beneath the Emotional Triad and known as Victory. It is the sephirah that helps in breaking down barriers, overcoming hardships, and managing intentions. Netsach depicts beating the odds and conquering obstacles, represented by the color purple.

8. Hod is part of the Instinctual Triad and Magical Triangle, also known as Surrender. It is the sephirah that encourages acceptance, capitulation, and acknowledgment of limitations. Hod depicts knowing when to give up and allowing things to happen on their own, represented by the color orange.

9. Yesod is part of the Instinctual Triad and Magical Triangle, also known as Foundation. It is the sephirah involved in telling the truth, discerning lies, and trustworthiness. Yesod depicts honesty, authenticity, and diligence, represented by the color green.

10. Malkuth is the lowest of the sephirot, also known as Sovereignty. It is the final stop on the Tree of Life, as the energy flow from Keter through the pathways culminates in Malkuth. This involves transforming from an abstract idea, concept, or matter to a *concrete expression* of these things. Malkuth is what manifests at the end of the journey or the actualized expression of the path, represented by the color brown.

The Kabbalistic Paths

The Kabbalistic Tree of Life contains a total of 32 possible mystical paths to discovering the secret wisdom imparted by the emanations of Ein Sof. These mystical paths include the 10 sephirot and the 22 Hebrew letter paths between them that connect everything together. In order to fully realize the meaning of the Tree of Life and its divine power, you must carefully study the sephirot and their Hebrew letter paths, discerning how they fit together. There is a strong correlation between the Hebrew alphabet and the spiritual energy of the sephirot, giving the Hebrew letters a mystical connotation within the Tree of Life.

Divine Language

Kabbalah is considered one of the four divine languages used in the Torah, with the others being Aggadah, Halachah, and Tanach. Human beings can achieve the capability to communicate with God through the use of divine languages. The actions of Moses are seen as an ideal example of discovering the ability to speak with the Divine Creator, and it is believed that all those who follow in his footsteps can eventually learn to do the same. Unlike the other divine languages, Kabbalah also contains a mystical aspect, hiding esoteric secrets that must be studied closely for many years before you can engage with them. Practitioners maintain that the letters and words of the Hebrew alphabet possess mystical qualities, and these properties can be wielded to unlock the occult knowledge connected to the divine.

The Hebrew Alphabet

The Sefer Yetzirah, written by Abraham 3,800 years ago, suggests that the letters of the Hebrew alphabet serve as the building blocks of the universe, embodying the divine energy of the Creator and the intelligence behind His creations. This includes every planet, moon, star, galaxy, and other cosmic phenomenon. Each month is associated with both a sign of the zodiac and a planet, the moon, or the sun. They are also all linked to a specific letter from the Hebrew alphabet. According to the Book of Formation, meditation exercises on the Hebrew letter connected to the current month can positively influence the events that occur during the month.

The 22 Hebrew Letter Paths

The 22 paths marked with letters from the Hebrew alphabet that connect the sephirot of the Tree of Life each have a specific meaning and mystical power.

א **Aleph:** The first letter of the Hebrew alphabet. It means "oneness with God," being a symbol of unity and the origin point from which all creation arises. This letter is associated with the concept of Divine Nothingness, as well as Ein Sof, which represents God's infinite and unknowable nature. Aleph is also the first letter in the three words used for the mystical name of God – אהיה אשר אהיה, pronounced as ʻehye ʻăšer ʻehye (Hebrew is read from right to left) – a translation of the phrase "I Am who I Am," which was the answer given to Moses in the Book of Exodus when he asked for God's true name.

ב **Bet:** The second letter of the Hebrew alphabet. It is associated with the concept of Binah, the third sephirah on the Tree of Life. This letter can be considered the feminine aspect of the divine, sometimes called the "Great Mother" or "Great Sea," and it has a connection with intellect and understanding. Bet also represents the ability to discern and differentiate between different matters and ideas, bringing a sense of cohesion or binding to the origins of creation. It symbolizes the foundation of the universe and the force known as the Divine Will, which brings everything into existence.

א **Gimel:** The third letter of the Hebrew alphabet. It evokes Chesed, the fourth sephirah on the Tree of Life. This letter possesses the attributes of love, kindness, and compassion, considered to be the source of all benevolence and positive actions. Gimel symbolizes God's grace and generosity and an association with the concepts of endowment and energy flow. Universal abundance and prosperity originate from the attributes of Gimel, which is also the source of all blessings and generosity in the world.

ד **Dalet:** The fourth letter of the Hebrew alphabet. It is connected to Geburah, the fifth sephirah on the Tree of Life. This letter possesses the attributes of strength, discipline, and judgment, being considered the source of all boundaries, laws, and limitations. Dalet can also be referred to as the Might or Power, expressing the justice of God. The idea of control and restriction is imbued in Dalet, representing the origin of structure and order within the universe. It symbolizes Divine Justice, embodying the concepts of fairness and righteousness.

ה **He:** The fifth letter of the Hebrew alphabet. It is associated with Tiferet, the sixth sephirah on the Tree of Life. This letter contains the attributes of balance, harmony, and beauty, the origin of all integration and balance in the universe. It is called the Glory or Beauty, expressing God's compassion and mercy. He is connected to the idea of Divine Compassion, from which compassion and beauty spring forth throughout the world.

ו **Vav:** The sixth letter of the Hebrew alphabet. It is linked to Netsach, the seventh sephirah on the Tree of Life. This letter has the characteristics of victory, endurance, and persistence and is the source of all-natural instincts and processes. Vav can be viewed as the Eternity or Victory, connected to the idea of an eternal and enduring God. It is also known as Divine Endurance, serving as the root of the world's victories and perseverance.

ז **Zayin:** The seventh letter of the Hebrew alphabet. It connects with Hod, the eighth sephirah on the Tree of Life. This letter symbolizes humility, surrender, and giving thanks. Submission and surrendering to God's will are major components of Zayin. It also has connotations of splendor, majesty, and humility, particularly as a part of God. Zayin embraces the acknowledgment of weakness or failure, avoiding the trap of allowing confidence to become arrogant. It can be considered Divine Humility, the source of giving yourself over to God's will.

ח **Het:** The eighth letter of the Hebrew alphabet. It embodies Yesod, the ninth sephirah on the Tree of Life. This letter is associated with the concepts of foundation, connection, and stability. Het can be called the Foundation or the Link to God, the different realms of existence. There is also an association with congruence and balance across the universe. It is the Divine Connectivity, possessing the building blocks needed for the spiritual and physical components of the world.

ט **Tet:** The ninth letter of the Hebrew alphabet. It is coupled with Malkuth, the tenth and final sephirah on the Tree of Life. This letter epitomizes kingship, sovereignty, and the physical world. Tet, also known as the Kingdom of Queen, is considered the source of physical manifestations within reality. It references God as the ultimate ruler of all things and the highest authority in the universe. The letter Tet expresses the idea of Divine Sovereignty, in which everything in existence falls under the dominion of God.

י **Yod:** The tenth letter of the Hebrew alphabet. It is considered to be the most spiritually powerful and mystical of the letters, maintaining a strong connection to Keter, the first and highest sephirah on the Tree of Life. This letter is linked to both spiritual and divine awareness. Yod can be called the Crown or Will, where God exists as the utmost spiritual reality and the wellspring of resolve and intention. It is considered the Divine Will, expressing all designs and spiritual awareness in the universe.

כ **Kaf:** The eleventh letter of the Hebrew alphabet. It is associated with Chochmah, the second sephirah on the Tree of Life. This letter symbolizes wisdom, intuition, and the origins of creation. Kaf is where creative ideas and intellectual understanding stems, also known as the Wisdom or Supernal Father. The beginning of the universe and spiritual intuition come from here. The letter Kaf represents Divine Wisdom and is considered the place where all worldly wisdom and understanding come from.

ל **Lamed:** The twelfth letter of the Hebrew alphabet. A goad, pastoral staff, shepherd's crook, or cattle prod sometimes represents Lamed. Like Bet, it is associated with Binah and the idea of Divine Understanding. This letter personifies the world's shared empathy, understanding, and comprehension.

מ Mem: The thirteenth letter of the Hebrew alphabet. It is coupled with Da'at, the third sephirah on the Tree of Life. This letter contains the characteristics of familiarity, consciousness, and self-awareness. Mem exemplifies spiritual insight, cognizance, and wisdom, referred to as Knowledge or Awareness. Known as Divine Knowledge, it can be considered the source of mindfulness, intellect, and sensibility throughout the universe.

נ Nun: The fourteenth letter of the Hebrew alphabet. It is related to Neshamah, one of the five parts of the soul, which consists of morality and emotion. This letter pertains to the attributes of spiritual awareness, divine inspiration, and a deep connection to God. Nun is called the Divine Soul or Spiritual Soul and is associated with Divine Inspiration, considered the source of all spiritual and divine influence worldwide.

ס Samekh: The fifteenth letter of the Hebrew alphabet. Like Het, it connects to Yesod, the ninth sephirah on the Tree of Life. This letter embodies the idea of support and infrastructure. It is an expression of the framework of the universe, which exists as part of the foundation of all things. Samekh is also associated with the idea of stability and structure, including the Divine Support that holds up the physical and metaphysical realms.

ע Ayin: The sixteenth letter of the Hebrew alphabet. It is associated with Hod, the eighth sephirah on the Tree of Life, just like the letter Zayin. Ayin embodies the traits of humility and gratitude, especially in relation to God's will. It is referred to as subservience or thankfulness, bowing to the majesty and splendor of the Divine Creator. This letter is also connected to Divine Acknowledgment, creating the opening through which you can give yourself over to the designs of the universe.

פ Pe: The seventeenth letter of the Hebrew alphabet. Kabbalistic scholarship maintains that the symbol for Pe is based on an open mouth, representing the fact that it follows Ayin, which forms a gateway into the divine by being the apparatus that actually brings the divine into reality. This is usually done through prayer, recitation of the sacred texts, and transfer of divine knowledge. It can be roughly translated as speech, vocalization, or breath and is related to Divine Expression.

צ Tsadi: The eighteenth letter of the Hebrew alphabet. It was given its name and symbol due to its resemblance to a fishing hook. This letter can be defined as hunting, capturing, or snaring. The shape of Tsadi can also be viewed as a person bowing in exaltation, conveying that you must humble yourself before the Divine Creator to glory in His works. It represents a righteous person, a faithful servant to God, and the Divine Worshipper.

ק **Qof:** The nineteenth letter of the Hebrew alphabet. It embodies the cyclical nature of the universe and everything therein. This is expressed through the eternal repetition of things like the changing seasons, the life cycles of humans, animals, and plants, as well as the ever-changing and repeating chains of celestial bodies. Just as everything within the natural world experiences birth, growth, decline, death, and rebirth, so too do the planets and stars. Qof also possesses the symbolic action of removing any negative coverings or husks so that the unfettered holiness hidden beneath it can be revealed. It is considered the Divine Wheel, constantly turning over from one aspect of the world to another.

ר **Resh:** The twentieth letter of the Hebrew alphabet. Despite falling near the end of the alphabet, Resh means "beginning" or "head." This letter denotes the idea that "the beginning of wisdom is the fear of God." It is associated with the choice between nobility, decadence, selflessness, and greed. The belief that you should be a leader instead of a follower by emulating the Divine Creator is also connected to Resh.

ש **Shin:** The twenty-first letter of the Hebrew alphabet. It translates to the word "tooth," and its symbol depicts the three pillars of flame. This letter has a strong association with fire, particularly in its function as a purification method. It also represents the fire of God and the divine energy that can cleanse and purify the soul. Shin embodies renewal and balance, with the letter's shape showing the two opposing extremes with the left and right pillars of flame, tempered by the third pillar of flame in the center. It is characterized as Divine Transformation, which sits at the root of all change throughout the universe.

ת **Tav:** The twenty-second and final letter of the Hebrew alphabet. It is defined as a sign, mark, or omen and the symbol of transcendence, fulfillment, and truth. This letter is connected to the concept of restoration, including restoring your spiritual essence to the Divine Creator. The entire universe emanated from God, and the course of its existence leads up to the moment of complete perfection. Since Tav is the last letter in the alphabet, it is followed by a return to the beginning. It is representative of Divine Emanation, containing both the origins and totality of the universe.

Chapter 3: Spheres, Planets, and Stars

The Kabbalistic Tree of Life and its sephirot are associated with astrology through the correlation between the various paths of the Tree of Life and notable celestial bodies. Sephirot and the astrological planets converge to create a complex tapestry of traits, characteristics, symbols, behaviors, spiritual essences, and meanings. Different sephirot match up with certain planets or other celestial bodies, signs of the zodiac, elements, astrological numbers, and Judaic angels and demons. Since it was through the emanations of God that the sephirot, planets, moons, and stars were all created, they possess the mystical and spiritual energies that permeate both the seen and unseen aspects of the universe.

Different planets are matched with sephirot.
Lsmpascal, CC BY-SA 3.0 <https://creativecommons.org/licenses/by-sa/3.0>, via Wikimedia Commons https://commons.wikimedia.org/wiki/File:Size_planets_comparison.jpg

The Astrological Planets

In the context of astrology, astrological planets refer to the planets within our solar system (excluding Earth), as well as the Sun and Moon. Note that while Pluto was downgraded to a "dwarf planet" by the International Astronomical Union (IAU) in 2006, it is still considered a regular planet within astrology. Each astrological planet is associated with specific characteristics and influences that can determine your actions and personality. The placement of the planets in your natal chart is believed to indicate your potential for having certain traits and for experiences to occur in your life. The list of astrological planets and their associations include:

The Sun: Associated with the self, the ego, and one's sense of identity. It is also connected to leadership, ambition, and vitality.

The Moon: Associated with emotions, instincts, and the unconscious mind. It is also connected to the mother, home, and security.

Mercury: Associated with communication, intelligence, and adaptability. It is also connected to travel and transportation.

Venus: Associated with love, beauty, and harmony. It is also connected to money and material possessions.

Mars: Associated with energy, aggression, and determination. It is also connected to sexuality and physical activity.

Jupiter: Associated with expansion, optimism, and good luck. It is also connected to higher education and philosophy.

Saturn: Associated with restriction, discipline, and responsibility. It is also connected to career and long-term goals.

Uranus: Associated with innovation, change, and rebellion. It is also connected to technology and the future.

Neptune: Associated with mysticism, illusion, and spirituality. It is also connected to art and imagination.

Pluto: Associated with transformation, power, and regeneration. It is also connected to sex and death.

The Sephirot and the Astrological Planets

The sephirot are all ruled by certain astrological planets possessing shared aspects and characteristics between them. Each planet (excluding Earth), the Sun, the Moon, and the four elements can be connected with a sephirah, notable symbol, defining trait, astrological number, color, flower, gemstone, angel, demon, and sign of the zodiac. The specific meaning of these characteristics helps to flesh out the connections made by the sephirot in the Tree of Life. It can all be taken as pieces of a larger puzzle, and you can observe the links by understanding the following:

The Sun

Sephirah: Tiferet
Symbol: Butterfly
Trait: Beauty
Number: 1
Color: Yellow
Flower: Sunflower
Gemstone: Ruby
Angel: Michael
Demon: Mammon
Zodiac Sign: Aries

The Moon

Sephirah: Yesod
Symbol: Crescent
Trait: Foundation
Number: 2
Colors: White and Silver
Flower: Moonflower
Gemstones: Pearl or Moonstone
Angel: Gabriel
Demon: Belphegor
Zodiac Sign: Cancer

Mercury

Sephirah: Hod
Symbol: Coin
Trait: Splendor

Number: 5
Colors: Blue and Yellow
Flower: Lavender
Gemstone: Emerald
Angel: Raphael
Demon: Beelzebub
Zodiac Sign: Gemini

Venus

Sephirah: Netsach
Symbol: Ouroboros
Trait: Victory
Number: 6
Color: Green
Flower: Rose
Gemstone: Diamond
Angel: Haniel
Demon: Lucifer
Zodiac Sign: Taurus

Mars

Sephirah: Geburah
Symbol: Lion
Trait: Courage
Number: 9
Color: Red
Flower: Peruvian Lily
Gemstone: Bloodstone
Angel: Samael
Demon: Lilith
Zodiac Sign: Leo

Jupiter

Sephirah: Chesed
Symbol: Heart
Trait: Mercy
Number: 3
Color: Purple
Flower: Carnation
Gemstone: Yellow Sapphire
Angel: Zadkiel
Demon: Hismael
Zodiac Sign: Sagittarius

Saturn

Sephirah: Binah
Symbol: Scythe
Trait: Understanding
Number: 8
Color: Brown
Flower: Amaranth
Gemstone: Iolite
Angel: Cassiel
Demon: Zazel
Zodiac Sign: Capricorn

Uranus

Sephirah: Keter
Symbol: Crown
Trait: Willpower
Number: 4
Color: Pink
Flower: Primrose
Gemstone: Rose Quartz

Angel: Uriel
Demon: Asmodeus
Zodiac Sign: Libra

Neptune

Sephirah: Chochmah
Symbol: Trident
Trait: Wisdom
Number: 7
Color: Sea Blue
Flower: Water Lily
Gemstone: Topaz
Angel: Raziel
Demon: Barbas
Zodiac Signs: Pisces and Aquarius

Pluto

Sephirah: Da'at
Symbol: Owl
Trait: Knowledge
Number: 10
Color: Black
Flower: Narcissus
Gemstone: Onyx
Angel: Azrael
Demon: Hecate
Zodiac Sign: Scorpio

The Four Elements

Sephirah: Malkuth
Symbols: Earth, Air, Fire, Water
Trait: Sovereignty
Number: 0

Colors: Brown
Flower: Daisy
Gemstones: Agate (Earth), Amethyst (Air), Citrine (Fire), Opal (Water)
Angel: Zuriel
Demon: Leviathan
Zodiac Sign: Virgo

Chapter 4: Through the Zodiac I. Cardinal Signs

In astrology, the zodiac is divided into 12 signs, each associated with one of the four cardinal directions: north, south, east, and west. The "cardinal signs" are the four signs that fall at the beginning of each season: Aries, Cancer, Libra, and Capricorn. They are considered the frontrunners to the rest of the zodiac and share a number of characteristics with one another. This includes assigning a specific element to each cardinal sign and a particularly significant day during its associated season. The elements are the four classical elements, corresponding to the four cardinal signs, and they connect to either solstices or equinoxes.

The cardinal signs also have an important role in Kabbalah. The energy of the sephirot on the Tree of Life is rooted in its connection to the zodiac, where the position and direction of celestial bodies and phenomena help inform the sephirot's influences. Depending on which ones are coupled with your own natal chart, the type of person you are, your attributes, and your path can all be traced back to both the sephirot and the zodiac. Anyone can benefit from learning more about themselves, especially if they have questions about aspects of their own life. It's another avenue for self-reflection and self-improvement that is necessary for you to continue growing.

Characteristics of the Zodiac Signs

Those connected to the cardinal signs are known to be strong leaders, often taking the initiative with things in their life. They are usually proactive, ready to step up and take charge of situations at any moment. People born under the cardinal signs are also ambitious, seeking to take a strategic approach when it comes to achieving their goals. They can be viewed as the "corners" of the zodiac, marking the beginning of a new season and a new growth cycle.

The Golden Dawn

The Hermetic Order of the Golden Dawn was a secret society primarily active around the late 19th and early 20th centuries. They were well-known for practicing ceremonial magic and delving into the occult and were originally founded using the teachings of Kabbalah and the Rosicrucians, an esoteric Christian fraternity that was part of a larger cultural movement in Europe involving spiritualism during the 17th century. The Golden Dawn was heavily influenced by the work of Eliphas Levi, an infamous British occultist, and the ceremonial magic used by the Hermetic Order of the Asiatic Brethren.

The Rose Cross represents the Golden Dawn.
Dm, CC0, via Wikimedia Commons
https://commons.wikimedia.org/wiki/File:Taro_Rose_Cross.svg

The Golden Dawn was founded in London in 1888 by Dr. William Robert Woodman, William Wynn Westcott, and Samuel Liddell MacGregor Mathers. All three were members of the Freemasons, and Freemasonry had a major impact on the Golden Dawn, especially in how it was set up with smaller, decentralized lodges, a hierarchy with increasing degrees to denote prominence, and secret, ritualistic initiation rites. However, unlike the Freemasons, they allowed women to become members and advance through the ranks on an equal footing with the men.

The Golden Dawn became one of the most influential occult organizations of its time, attracting many prominent members of the day. Some of their more notable recruits included the acclaimed Irish poet, writer, and dramatist William Butler Yeats, British author and Sherlock Holmes scribe Sir Arthur Conan Doyle, and the divisive English writer and occultist Aleister Crowley, who would later go on to find his own esoteric religion known as Thelema. Highly respected members of society, such as artists, writers, philosophers, and doctors, could be found among their ranks. During the Age of Enlightenment, when intellectualism, reason, and the push for empirical evidence spread throughout Europe, the Golden Dawn was an attractive alternative to traditional religions.

The organization had a hierarchical structure where members were initiated into various grades, each possessing its own set of teachings, rituals, and practices. There were three Orders that members could advance through, and each Order was broken down into grades with paired numbers. The paired numbers within each Order were related to positions on the Tree of Life. The Golden Dawn imparted knowledge on subjects like magic, alchemy, astrology, Tarot, and Kabbalah. It also focused on the development of psychic abilities, clairvoyance, and astral projection.

Despite the influential members within the Golden Dawn, it was officially dissolved as an organization in 1903. However, its teachings and practices still went on to have a significant impact on modern occultism and esotericism, even seeing some of them adopted by the very same traditions that inspired it. Many of its members also went on to form their own mystical and occult-centric organizations, carrying what they learned from the Golden Dawn into their new ventures. Contemporary esoteric groups, such as the Hermetic Brotherhood of Luxor, can trace their roots directly back to the Golden Dawn.

The Tetragrammaton

The Tetragrammaton is the four-letter name of the Hebrew God – YHWH – and it is considered the most sacred and holy name in all of Judaism. It is often referred to as the "ineffable name" or "unutterable name," as the Jewish people believed it was so holy that it should never be spoken out loud. Instead, the Hebrew word "Adonai," which means "Lord," is typically substituted for it when reading from the Hebrew Bible (also known in Christianity as the Old Testament). The exact pronunciation of the Tetragrammaton is "Jehovah" or "Yahweh." Although the name appears 6,828 times in the Hebrew Bible, the precise pronunciation has been lost to time, so nobody is certain how to say it correctly.

The Tetragrammaton.
https://openclipart.org/detail/307583/esoteric-staff-remix

In the context of Kabbalah, the Tetragrammaton is associated with the sephirah of Keter, the highest of the ten emanations of God and through which He created the entire universe. It also has a connection with the four elements, the four cardinal directions, and the four worlds of creation. The Tetragrammaton is central to the practice of theurgic magic, which uses special rituals and meditations to invoke the presence of God.

As with Judaism, the Tetragrammaton in Christianity is seen as the original name of God. Jesus is considered the embodiment of the name, being sent to Earth by God to execute His will in the form of a mortal man. The Tetragrammaton is not used in Islam, but Allah, their name for God, is viewed as sacred and sits above all other names for Him. Because the Tetragrammaton is considered a very sacred and holy name in Judaism, there are strict religious rules and customs regarding its use and pronunciation. Even writing the word "God" is regarded as taboo, so many sections of Jewish culture will instead replace the "o" in God with a dash, rendering it as "G-d."

Characteristics of the Cardinal Signs

In addition to the traditional Kabbalistic version of cardinal signs, both the Golden Dawn and the Tetragrammaton have traits and characteristics intrinsically linked to them. The primary attributes associated with the four cardinal signs include:

Aries

Aries is the first sign of the zodiac and the first cardinal sign. It marks the beginning of the astrological year and is associated with the energy of initiation, leadership, and action. Those born under Aries are said to be ambitious and confident, always eager to take on new challenges and explore new horizons.

Zodiac Symbol: The Ram

Cardinal Direction: East

Seasonal Day: Vernal Equinox (start of spring)

Sephirah: Geburah

Kabbalistic Path: Netsach to Yesod

Ruling Planet: Mars

Element: Fire

Key Concept: Initiative

Energy Type: Masculine

Hebrew Month: Nisan

Hebrew Letters: He and Dalet

Tetragrammaton Letters: He-Vav-He-Yod (יהוה)

Guiding Angel: Malahidael

Major Arcana Tarot Card: The Emperor

Minor Arcana Tarot Cards: 2, 3, 4 of Wands

Number: 44

Color: Red

Day: Tuesday

Wood: Dogwood

Metal: Steel or Iron

Flower: Geranium, Sweetpea, or Daisy

Herb: Thistle

Essential Oils: Frankincense, Pine, and Neroli

Gemstone: Diamond

Power Stone: Ruby

Cancer

Cancer is the fourth sign of the zodiac and the second cardinal sign. It is associated with the energy of nurturing, emotional intelligence, and family. Those born with Cancer are said to be deeply sensitive, intuitive, and protective of those about whom they care.

Zodiac Symbol: The Crab

Cardinal Direction: North

Seasonal Day: Summer Solstice (start of summer)

Sephirah: Yesod

Kabbalistic Path: Binah to Geburah

Ruling Planet: The Moon

Element: Water

Key Concept: Receptivity

Energy Type: Feminine

Hebrew Month: Tammuz

Hebrew Letters: Tav-Het

Tetragrammaton Letters: He-Vav-He-Yod (יהוה)

Guiding Angel: Muriel

Major Arcana Tarot Card: The Chariot

Minor Arcana Tarot Cards: 2, 3, 4 of Cups

Number: 69

Color: Yellow-Orange

Day: Monday

Wood: Holly

Metal: Silver

Flower: Jasmine or Gardenia

Herb: Honeysuckle

Essential Oils: Myrrh and Chamomile

Gemstone: Chriscola

Power Stones: Moonstone and Emerald

Libra

Libra is the seventh sign of the zodiac and the third cardinal sign. It is associated with the energy of balance, harmony, and diplomacy. Those born under Libra are said to be charming, cooperative, and tactful, able to bring people together and mediate conflicts.

Zodiac Symbol: The Scales

Cardinal Direction: West

Seasonal Day: Autumnal Equinox (start of autumn)

Sephirah: Netsach

Kabbalistic Path: Tiferet to Geburah

Ruling Planet: Venus

Element: Air

Key Concept: Harmony

Energy Type: Masculine

Hebrew Month: Tishrei

Hebrew Letters: Lamed-Pe

Tetragrammaton Letters: Vav-He-Yod-He (והיה)

Guiding Angel: Zuriel

Major Arcana Tarot Card: Justice

Minor Arcana Tarot Cards: 2, 3, 4 of Swords

Number: 33

Color: Green

Day: Friday

Wood: Poplar

Metal: Copper

Flower: Rose

Herb: Thyme

Essential Oils: Sandalwood, Rose, and Clary

Gemstone: Opal

Power Stone: Diamond

Capricorn

Capricorn is the tenth sign of the zodiac and the fourth cardinal sign. It is associated with the energy of structure, responsibility, and ambition. Those born under Capricorn are said to be disciplined, hardworking, and goal-oriented, capable of setting and achieving objectives through determination and focus.

Zodiac Symbol: The Goat

Cardinal Direction: South

Seasonal Day: Winter Solstice (start of winter)

Sephirah: Binah

Kabbalistic Path: Hod to Tiferet

Ruling Planet: Saturn

Element: Earth

Key Concept: Structure

Energy Type: Feminine

Hebrew Month: Tevet

Hebrew Letters: Bet-Ayin

Tetragrammaton Letters: He-Yod-He-Vav (היהו)

Guiding Angel: Hanael

Major Arcana Tarot Card: The Devil

Minor Arcana Tarot Cards: 2, 3, 4 of Pentacles

Number: 23

Color: Blue-Violet

Day: Saturday

Wood: Birch

Metal: Lead

Flower: Carnation

Herb: Comfrey Root

Essential Oils: Juniper, Chamomile, Cedarwood, Spearmint, and Fennel

Gemstone: Onyx

Power Stone: Quartz Crystal

Chapter 5: Through the Zodiac II. Fixed Signs

The fixed signs of the zodiac are Taurus, Leo, Scorpio, and Aquarius. These signs are known for their determination and stability. They are considered "fixed" because they possess a fixed modality characterized by persistence, determination, and a strong sense of purpose. Fixed signs can be considered the stabilizers of the zodiac, taking the enthusiastic, creative ideas of the cardinal signs and turning them into something concrete and realistically applicable.

Characteristics of the Fixed Signs

As with the cardinal signs, the traditional Kabbalistic version of fixed signs also has traits and characteristics connected to the Golden Dawn and the Tetragrammaton. The primary attributes associated with the four fixed signs include:

Taurus

Taurus is the second sign of the zodiac and the first fixed sign. It is associated with the material world, including money, possessions, and physical pleasure. Those born under Taurus are said to be loyal, reliable, stubborn, and realistic in matters of the world.

Zodiac Symbol: The Bull

Seasonal Day: May Day (middle of spring)

Sephirah: Nesach
Kabbalistic Path: Chochmah to Chesed
Ruling Planet: Venus
Element: Earth
Key Concept: Stability
Energy Type: Feminine
Hebrew Month: Iyar
Hebrew Letters: Vav-Pe
Tetragrammaton Letters: Yod-He-He-Vav (יההו)
Guiding Angel: Asmodel
Major Arcana Tarot Card: The Hierophant
Minor Arcana Tarot Cards: 5, 6, 7 of Pentacles
Number: 42
Color: Red-Orange
Day: Friday
Wood: Willow
Metal: Copper
Flower: Narcissus
Herb: Sage
Essential Oils: Rose, Patchouli, and Lilac
Gemstone: Emerald
Power Stone: Agate

Leo

Leo is the fifth sign of the zodiac and the second fixed sign. It is associated with strength, creativity, self-expression, and leadership. Those born under Leo are said to be passionate, theatrical, protective, and generous.

Zodiac Symbol: The Lion
Seasonal Day: Midsummer (middle of summer)
Sephirah: Tiferet
Kabbalistic Path: Geburah to Chesed
Ruling Planet: The Sun
Element: Fire

Key Concept: Magnetism

Energy Type: Masculine

Hebrew Month: Av

Hebrew Letters: Tet-Kaf

Tetragrammaton Letters: He-Vav-Yod-He (הויה)

Guiding Angel: Verchiel

Major Arcana Tarot Card: Strength

Minor Arcana Tarot Cards: 5, 6, 7 of Wands

Number: 9

Color: Yellow

Day: Sunday

Wood: Hazel

Metal: Gold

Flower: Sunflower or Marigold

Herb: St. John's Wort

Essential Oils: Cinnamon, Cedar, and Orange

Gemstone: Ruby

Power Stone: Amber

Scorpio

Scorpio is the eighth sign of the zodiac and the third fixed sign. It is associated with intensity, depth, and transformation. Those born under Scorpio are said to be honest, ambitious, temperamental, and have a strategic mind.

Zodiac Symbol: The Scorpion

Seasonal Day: Sukkot (middle of autumn)

Sephirah: Da'at

Kabbalistic Path: Tiferet to Netsach

Ruling Planet: Pluto

Element: Water

Key Concept: Intensity

Energy Type: Feminine

Hebrew Month: Cheshvan

Hebrew Letters: Nun-Dalet

Tetragrammaton Letters: Vav-He-He-Yod (וההי)

Guiding Angel: Barbiel

Major Arcana Tarot Card: Death

Minor Arcana Tarot Cards: 5, 6, 7 of Cups

Number: 72

Color: Blue-Green

Day: Tuesday

Wood: Hemlock

Metal: Iron

Flower: Chrysanthemum

Herb: Wormwood

Essential Oils: Tuberose and Rosemary

Gemstone: Topaz

Power Stone: Garnet

Aquarius

Aquarius is the eleventh sign of the zodiac and the fourth fixed sign. It is associated with innovation, progress, and social change. Those born under Aquarius are said to be practical, forward-thinking, humanitarian, and capable of ingenious solutions to problems.

Zodiac Symbol: The Water Bearer

Seasonal Day: Midwinter (middle of winter)

Sephirah: Binah

Kabbalistic Path: Chochmah to Tiferet

Ruling Planet: Saturn

Element: Air

Key Concept: Eccentricity

Energy Type: Masculine

Hebrew Month: Shevat

Hebrew Letters: Bet-Tsadi

Tetragrammaton Letters: He-Yod-Vav-He (היוה)

Guiding Angel: Cambiel

Major Arcana Tarot Card: The Star
Minor Arcana Tarot Cards: 5, 6, 7 of Swords
Number: 51
Color: Violet
Day: Saturday
Wood: Ash
Metal: Aluminum
Flower: Orchid
Herb: Valerian
Essential Oils: Fennel Oil and Lemon Verbena
Gemstone: Amethyst
Power Stone: Sapphire

Chapter 6: Through the Zodiac III. Mutable Signs

The mutable signs of the zodiac are Gemini, Virgo, Sagittarius, and Pisces. They are considered flexible and adaptable, more capable of evolving than the other signs. Mutable signs come at the end of each season, presaging the transformation from one to another. These signs thrive on change but also have a restless nature, never wanting to stay in one place or do one thing for a long time. The mutable signs can take the ideas solidified by the fixed signs and whittle down the rougher edges, perfecting them.

Characteristics of the Mutable Signs

Like with the cardinal and fixed signs, the traditional Kabbalistic version of mutable signs also have traits and characteristics connected to the Golden Dawn and the Tetragrammaton. The primary attributes associated with the four mutable signs include:

Gemini

Gemini is the third sign of the zodiac and the first mutable sign. It is associated with communication, information, and duality. Those born under Gemini are said to be cunning, perceptive, adaptable, contrarian, and can easily navigate most social situations.

Zodiac Symbol: The Twins

Seasonal Transition: End of spring to start of summer

Sephirah: Hod

Kabbalistic Path: Binah to Tiferet

Ruling Planet: Mercury

Element: Air

Key Concept: Variety

Energy Type: Masculine

Hebrew Month: Sivan

Hebrew Letters: Zayin-Resh

Tetragrammaton Letters: Yod-Vav-He-He (יוהה)

Guiding Angel: Ambriel

Major Arcana Tarot Card: The Lovers

Minor Arcana Tarot Cards: 8, 9, 10 of Swords

Number: 14

Color: Orange

Day: Wednesday

Wood: Oak

Metal: Mercury

Flower: Violets

Herb: Parsley

Essential Oils: Lavender, Lemongrass, and Benzoin

Gemstone: Agate

Power Stone: Aquamarine

Virgo

Virgo is the sixth sign of the zodiac and the second mutable sign. It is associated with order, intelligence, discernment, and craftsmanship. Those born under Virgo are said to be detail-oriented, have plenty of common sense, and often take up career paths where they perform service, such as in the military, clerical jobs, government positions, and manual labor.

Zodiac Symbol: The Virgin

Seasonal Transition: End of summer to start of autumn

Sephirah: Hod

Kabbalistic Path: Tiferet to Chesed

Ruling Planet: Mercury

Element: Earth

Key Concept: Perfection

Energy Type: Feminine

Hebrew Month: Elul

Hebrew Letters: Yod-Resh

Tetragrammaton Letters: He-He-Vav-Yod (ההוי)

Guiding Angel: Hamaliel

Major Arcana Tarot Card: The Hermit

Minor Arcana Tarot Cards: 8, 9, 10 of Pentacles

Number: 5

Color: Yellow-Green

Day: Wednesday

Wood: Aspen

Metal: Pewter

Flower: Morning Glory

Herb: Dill

Essential Oils: Lemon Balm, Caraway, and Sage

Gemstone: Peridot

Power Stone: Amethyst

Sagittarius

Sagittarius is the ninth sign of the zodiac and the third mutable sign. It is associated with philosophy, exploration, abstract intelligence, and higher education. Those born under Sagittarius are said to be adventurous, optimistic, and clever – and have a deep appreciation for nature.

Zodiac Symbol: The Archer

Seasonal Transition: End of autumn to start of winter

Sephirah: Chesed

Kabbalistic Path: Tiferet to Geburah

Ruling Planet: Jupiter

Element: Fire

Key Concept: Expansion

Energy Type: Masculine

Hebrew Month: Kislev

Hebrew Letters: Gimel-Samekh

Tetragrammaton Letters: Vav-Yod-He-He (ויהה)

Guiding Angel: Advachiel

Major Arcana Tarot Card: Temperance

Minor Arcana Tarot Cards: 8, 9, 10 of Wands

Number: 65

Color: Blue

Day: Thursday

Wood: Elder

Metal: Tin

Flower: Iris

Herb: Chicory

Essential Oils: Clove, Juniper Berry, and Vetiver

Gemstone: Turquoise

Power Stone: Lapis Lazuli

Pisces

Pisces is the twelfth sign of the zodiac and the fourth mutable sign. It is associated with imagination, compassion, spirituality, and unconditional love. Those born under Pisces are said to be artistic, empathetic, naïve, and possess a sense of idealism.

Zodiac Symbol: The Fish

Seasonal Transition: End of winter to start of spring

Sephirah: Chochmah

Kabbalistic Path: Netsach to Malkuth

Ruling Planet: Neptune

Element: Water

Key Concept: Compassion

Energy Type: Feminine

Hebrew Month: Adar

Hebrew Letters: Gimel-Qof

Tetragrammaton Letters: He-He-Yod-Vav (ההיו)
Guiding Angel: Barchiel
Major Arcana Tarot Card: The Moon
Minor Arcana Tarot Cards: 8, 9, 10 of Cups
Number: 34
Color: Violet-Red
Day: Thursday
Wood: Wild Olive
Metal: Platinum
Flower: Hyacinth
Herb: Yarrow
Essential Oils: Gardenia, Camphor, and Jasmine
Gemstone: Aquamarine
Power Stone: Tourmaline

Chapter 7: Lessons of the Lunar Nodes

The lunar nodes play an important role in Kabbalistic astrology. This stems from their astronomical significance, as whenever a full moon is close enough to one of the lunar nodes, there will be a lunar eclipse, and when a new moon is near them, a solar eclipse will occur. They can also influence the ocean's tides, causing them to become lower than usual. However, due to global warming and the rising sea level, the precession of lunar nodes will likely contribute to an increase in coastal flooding by the 2030s.

The Lunar Nodes

Lunar nodes are the two points in space where the moon's orbit intersects the plane of Earth's orbit around the sun, also known as the ecliptic plane. The point where the moon moves north of the ecliptic plane is called the ascending node, and the point where it moves south of the ecliptic plane is called the descending node. In astrology, the lunar nodes are considered important points in your natal chart and are often used to interpret these charts.

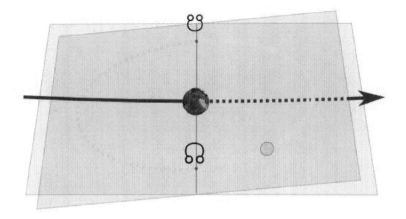

The north and south lunar nodes.

Episcophagus, CC BY-SA 4.0 <https://creativecommons.org/licenses/by-sa/4.0>, via Wikimedia Commons https://commons.wikimedia.org/wiki/File:Lunar_nodes.svg

Lunar Precession

Lunar precession is the gradual change in the orientation of the moon's rotational axis in space. It is caused by the gravitational pull of the sun and the Earth on the moon's equatorial bulge, causing the moon's axis to move in a small circle. This movement, called precession, impacts the moon's poles by pointing them in slightly different directions over time. The precession of the moon's rotational axis will result in an alteration to the moon's apparent position in the sky, which is something that can be observed over a period of 18.6 years. This is known as the lunar nodal cycle. The precession of the moon also affects the position of the lunar nodes since they are determined by the location where the orbit of the moon crosses the ecliptic.

The North (Ascending) Node

The north or ascending node is the point in the orbit of the moon where it moves from the southern hemisphere of the sky to the northern hemisphere, as viewed from the Earth. It represents the types of experiences you need to cultivate to improve your karma and evolve spiritually. In Kabbalistic astrology, the north node is also called the *tikkun*. It is considered the karmic adjustment your soul needs to carry out before it can grow. Your tikkun aids your personal development and brings forth new opportunities. It symbolizes the beginning of your journey when you are still inexperienced and have plenty of progress yet to be made.

The South (Descending) Node

The south or descending node is the point in the moon's orbit where it crosses over from the northern hemisphere of the sky to the southern hemisphere from the vantage point of Earth. It represents the traits and experiences that come naturally to you. However, they may be overdeveloped and serve as a crutch that you fall back on since they tend to be within your comfort zone. In Kabbalistic astrology, the south node is considered a point of release, where you must let go of old habits, attachments, and behaviors. It is associated with karmic patterns and symbolizes the people, places, things, and events you need to part from to develop as an individual.

Kabbalah and the Lunar Nodes

Regarding Kabbalistic astrology, the lunar nodes can help you answer important questions about your destiny, karmic path, and identities in past lives. You can find out why you exist, what you're meant to do with your life, and where you should focus your energy. The different combinations of north and south nodes will create a unique set of characteristics, destinies, and incarnations that you can use to help guide you when determining your future.

Combinations of the North and South Nodes

Although the north and south nodes are completely opposite from one another, they can work together when combined to establish a specific group of characteristics that will move to the forefront. These combinations include:

North Node in Aries and South Node in Libra

Life: You need to learn how to become more self-reliant, as you have a tendency to place all of your focus on your current relationships. Don't let your partnerships define you; you have plenty of great attributes as an individual. Move on from any toxic situations you're involved in, as it isn't worth the harm it does to your being. While relationships require a lot of work, you have to be secure with yourself before you can put in the effort necessary to sustain them.

Destiny: You are on a journey of self-discovery and will be a pioneer with your ideas.

Incarnation: In a past life, you were driven and self-sufficient. You were likely an ambitious and successful person in your professional life, but your relationships might have suffered because of it. Use your current life to work on improving your relationships with others, but don't allow them to consume you.

North Node in Taurus and South Node in Scorpio

Life: You enjoy the finer things in life, but you can also be too generous and hedonistic. You're likely in charge of your family's finances rather than your partner. Maintaining consistency in the flow of your emotions and keeping promises is essential since you tend to be too focused on personal evolution. Don't put up too many walls; it's okay to let others in, especially someone as trusted as a romantic partner.

Destiny: You are on a journey of experiencing a sharing of resources with a spouse or partner and building your wealth on your own terms.

Incarnation: In a past life, you were fiercely independent, never relying on anyone else to help you out with anything. However, you may have become too greedy, losing sight of what's truly important. Use your current life to balance your personal and professional lives, finding a comfortable medium between both aspects of your existence.

North Node in Gemini and South Node in Sagittarius

Life: You are an independent thinker and possess great communication skills. Whether it's through speaking or writing, you say what you mean and rely on facts to get your point across. Seeing new places and meeting new people is your favorite activity, and you enjoy a challenge. After all your diverse experiences, you will return enriched and ready to pass on all that you've learned to others.

Destiny: You are on a journey of discovering new and exciting things worldwide and using your own experiences to communicate the lessons learned to those in an earlier phase of their lives.

Incarnation: In a past life, you were an explorer or adventurer and often spoke about your experiences as a great orator or author. Use your current life to learn about the world and share these ideas without forgetting to return home.

North Node in Cancer and South Node in Capricorn

Life: You constantly struggle between your professional career and your growing family. Sometimes, you can be too ambitious, forgetting to cultivate relationships with people outside of work. Focusing on your job is a way to cope with problems in your life, leading you to neglect the other facets of your world. Make sure to also take care of your needs, giving yourself time to rest and recuperate.

Destiny: You are journeying to nurture your private and professional lives so they can both be fulfilling. In a tug-of-war between the two, it's likely that the family side will come out on top.

Incarnation: In a past life, you were overly invested in your career, and your romantic and familial relationships suffered for it. Use your current life to learn how to be emotionally sensitive to the needs of others. This can take your relationships to a new level.

North Node in Leo and South Node in Aquarius

Life: Artistic and creative endeavors are your bread and butter. You tend to be a dreamer, and while this doesn't always result in realistic goals, reaching for the stars can sometimes work out for you. While you prefer to be part of a group or team, you rarely take on a leadership role. You long to be noticed, but you're uncomfortable in the spotlight. However, once you've seen how people respond to your talents, it will become easier to step outside your comfort zone and shine.

Destiny: You are on a journey of creative expression, seeking to make a name for yourself in the world of arts and entertainment. It's a difficult road to walk, but if you stick with it and believe in yourself, you might just go the distance.

Incarnation: In a past life, you were brimming with creativity but hesitant to take a chance. You played it safe and stuck with an unglamorous career as a safety net. Use your current life to learn how to take the reins, which can elevate you to new heights.

North Node in Virgo and South Node in Pisces

Life: You are a nurturer, always looking to heal the hurts of others. However, you must first heal yourself before you can be as effective as possible. Some of your ideas are a bit too extreme and are unlikely to ever move from the realms of fantasy into reality. This doesn't mean giving up on your dreams – it just means you must manage your expectations. Keeping up with a routine and establishing positive daily habits can help you overcome your tendency to let things in the present slip by you while thinking about the future.

Destiny: You are on a journey of transformation. Look for opportunities to improve yourself, but never ignore your drive to help others in their own personal development.

Incarnation: In a past life, you were someone with many health issues. This has made you very empathetic to those in a similar situation, and you are sensitive to their physical and emotional needs. Use your current life to become more critical and assertive. Don't let people push you around because you show sympathy for others. While you have a tendency to disappear into the spiritual world, ignoring your own relationships, you have a chance to become more communicative.

North Node in Libra and South Node in Aries

Life: You are naturally independent, but you also tend to speak or act impulsively. Learning to work cooperatively and love others freely will be challenging, as you're used to putting your needs first. Now, you have to focus on others.

Destiny: You are on a journey of learning lessons about commitment in your relationships and partnerships. While you are a leader and self-reliant, you don't need to do everything by yourself.

Incarnation: In a past life, you were a lone wolf, working hard to ensure you never needed anyone else's help to survive. However, this cuts you off from the benefits of maintaining close relationships. Use your current life to learn how to be more diplomatic with others, showing a willingness to listen to their ideas instead of always forging ahead with your own.

North Node in Scorpio and South Node in Taurus

Life: You have a deep connection to the spiritual and metaphysical worlds. Because of this, you tend to rely on the support of others to help you survive, especially financially. Whether through receiving an inheritance or marrying a wealthy spouse, you have the freedom to focus your energy on things beyond putting food on the table and a roof over your head. You can sometimes become too obsessed with your current endeavors, and addiction is a very real danger for you.

Destiny: You are on a journey of spiritual enrichment, experiencing the mystical side of the world that most people ignore.

Incarnation: In a past life, you were a trust fund baby or stay-at-home spouse. Use your current life to improve your ability to manage your own affairs, and be patient when it comes to finding your path. Don't hesitate to trust your intuition. Let it help you navigate the treacherous waters and get you to a place where you don't feel controlled or trapped.

North Node in Sagittarius and South Node in Gemini

Life: You are a very talkative person, but you can sometimes lack focus. There is a constant drive within you to seek out wisdom from many different places, and you enjoy learning new things. However, you also tend to change from one subject to another the moment you start to become bored. You are easily distracted, yet when you can put your mind to it, you can find great success.

Destiny: You are on a journey of applying the wealth of knowledge you've accrued to practical purposes. Your generosity with others will come through both with resources and information.

Incarnation: In a past life, you were a teacher or philosopher. However, you remained stuck in the world of academia. Use your current life to take everything you've learned and try them out in the real world. Don't just talk about something – get out there and actually do it.

North Node in Capricorn and South Node in Cancer

Life: You are very pragmatic, seeking opportunities with the best chance of success. Your hard work and motivation stem from a need for approval, which you get quite frequently. In certain aspects of your life, you're an idealist and humanitarian, but you can also be a bit selfish and needy at times. Although you are very goal-oriented and strive to be the best at your chosen profession, you do not want to seek fame.

Destiny: You are pursuing personal fulfillment and finding a healthy work-life balance while pursuing your goals.

Incarnation: In a past life, you were a successful behind-the-scenes person. However, your ambitions were somewhat limited by your tendency to avoid taking too many risks. Use your current life to branch out and set some goals which may seem out of reach. You might just surprise yourself with your ability to achieve them, despite the smaller chance of success.

North Node in Aquarius and South Node in Leo

Life: You are the kind of person whose biggest desire is to leave the world a better place than you found it. When it comes to things like politics and governments, you usually take a more liberal or progressive stance. However, you also enjoy being the center of attention, and some of your efforts can come off as self-aggrandizing rather than humanitarian. Continue to develop as a person, and these issues will disappear in time.

Destiny: You are on a journey of social justice, giving a voice to the people who are too often forgotten by the rest of the world.

Incarnation: In a past life, you were a social activist, focusing a great deal on helping others and fighting for a cause. Use your current life to temper some of your more aggressive personality traits so you can learn how to negotiate and compromise in order to benefit everyone.

North Node in Pisces and South Node in Virgo

Life: You are someone that focuses on the big picture, undertaking endeavors that will initiate change for huge swathes of people. You can sometimes lack boundaries, as you're always pushing others to improve. Since you're a perfectionist, you expect that same level of commitment from the people around you.

Destiny: You are on a journey to change the world through visionary ideas or innovative actions.

Incarnation: In a past life, you were a scientist, doctor, or inventor on the cutting edge of science and technology. You constantly sought to improve on what came before, no matter how complacent others in your field might have become. Use your current life to relax a bit. While you can still push the envelope, take some time to find a calming hobby that doesn't require you to always be driving forward and putting in 110% effort.

Chapter 8: Reading the Kabbalistic Natal Chart

Now that you're better acquainted with the planets and zodiac signs, it's time to put all of that knowledge to good use and learn how to interpret a Kabbalistic natal chart. The stars, planets, and other celestial bodies can significantly affect you as a person, even if you don't realize it. Becoming more familiar with each aspect of a natal chart will make it easier to determine the best way to interpret the signs and other information it can provide.

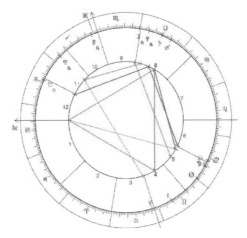

An example of a natal chart.

Mom, CC BY-SA 3.0 <https://creativecommons.org/licenses/by-sa/3.0>, via Wikimedia Commons https://commons.wikimedia.org/wiki/File:Natal_Chart_–_Adam.svg

What Is the Kabbalistic Natal Chart?

The Kabbalistic Natal Chart is a chart used in Kabbalistic astrology to understand the spiritual aspects of your life, including your soul's purpose, strengths, and challenges. It is believed that the chart can reveal the potential of your spiritual path and explain how you can best fulfill your purpose in life. The natal chart is created by analyzing the positions of the planets and other celestial bodies at the time of your birth and then interpreting them according to Kabbalistic principles.

The Astrological Houses

In astrology, the horoscope chart is divided into 12 astrological houses. These houses represent different areas of life and are determined by the time and location of a person's birth. Each house corresponds to a different zodiac sign and planet, and these astrological symbols provide insight into various aspects of someone's life, such as their career, relationships, family, and health. Each house also has a natural ruling planet, which is the planet that governs the affairs of the house and is considered to be the strongest planet in that house.

The 12 houses are usually depicted on a wheel, with the 1st house set around 9:00 and each subsequent house found by moving counter-clockwise. The 1st through 6th houses are the personal houses. They govern a person's private life; those born under these may have trouble moving on from their childhood home or friends. The 7th through 12th houses are the interpersonal houses. They rule a person's relationships; those born under these may tend to leave the past behind. These houses and their descriptions include:

1st House (Aries): House of Self

The 1st House, also called the Ascendant or Rising Sign, represents the self, personality, physical appearance, first impressions, and a general outlook on life. It is ruled by the planet Mars. Celestial bodies transiting into this house will let you see your ideas, viewpoints, and other endeavors solidify. Your goals will also finally be made manifest.

2nd House (Taurus): House of Possessions

The 2nd House represents material possessions, personal finances, daily routines, work ethic, and self-worth. It is ruled by the planet Venus. When celestial bodies transit into this house, it can shine a light on any changes to your self-esteem or personal resources. You tend to seek security through materialistic things, but you will also wear your emotions on your sleeve.

3rd House (Gemini): House of Communication

The 3rd House represents communication, social activities, siblings, neighbors, and short-distance travel. It is ruled by the planet Mercury. As celestial bodies transit into this house, you will find that critical information concerning those closest to you is revealed. Since communication is the best way to solve most problems, allowing for a strong foundation in relationships, focusing your energy on this part of your life can lead to greater success.

4th House (Cancer): House of Home and Family

The 4th House represents home, family, self-care, femininity, and emotional foundations. It is ruled by the Moon. Celestial bodies moving through this house will implore you to put time, money, and energy into building up your infrastructure. This includes establishing safe spaces and private sanctuaries where you can work on your relationships with family members.

5th House (Leo): House of Pleasure

The 5th House represents pleasure, creativity, joy, fertility, romance, and self-expression. It is ruled by the Sun. While celestial bodies transit through this house, you will find your creative inspiration boosted, and it can greatly increase your self-confidence. Find something that fulfills you and makes you feel satisfied, no matter what that might be.

6th House (Virgo): House of Health

The 6th House represents health, fitness, habits, organization, and self-value. It is ruled by the planet Mercury. Celestial bodies moving across this house will stimulate your ability to establish good habits and redefine your daily routines. Seek a balance between your home and work life, and be sure not to neglect your mental health. Where you spend your time is just as important as who you spend that time with, so make sure you have a healthy environment around you.

7th House (Libra): House of Partnership

The 7th House, also called the Descendant, represents partnerships, relationships, marriage, contracts, equality, and interpersonal skills. It is ruled by the planet Venus. When celestial bodies move across this house, you will find success in drawing up contracts and closing major deals. Your romantic relationships are just as important as your professional ones, so if you put in the same amount of effort into them, you will achieve a significant upgrade with your partner or spouse.

8th House (Scorpio): House of Transformation

The 8th House represents transformation, assets, shared resources, intimacy, joint ventures, and mystery. It is ruled by the planet Pluto. Celestial bodies transiting this house can aid you in navigating the complex situations you might find yourself in. While it's perfectly acceptable to indulge yourself, since nobody knows just how much time they have left on this Earth, remember to remain flexible regarding your interests. You should also be willing to forgive and forget past transgressions and learn not to cling to the successes of the past. Be ready to open yourself up to the here and now and the great things that can happen in the future.

9th House (Sagittarius): House of Philosophy

The 9th House represents philosophy, higher education, travel, law, religion, learning, and transcultural relations. It is ruled by the planet Jupiter. As celestial bodies transit into this house, you will delve into a new subject enthusiastically. While you might feel stuck in a rut with your current situation, you can shake off the cobwebs and reignite your passions by looking at things differently. Sometimes a change in scenery can do just as much to break you out of a dull routine as anything else.

10th House (Capricorn): House of Social Status

The 10th House represents social status, career, long-term goals, masculinity, fame, and reputation. It is ruled by the planet Saturn. As celestial bodies move through this house, you will find yourself making a change in your career and professional aspirations. There is also a chance that it can reveal someone hiding their ambitions, possibly seeking to succeed at your expense. Be careful with who you trust, especially regarding your reputation. While being popular is not everything in life, there's no reason to let your social status needlessly suffer.

11th House (Aquarius): House of Friendship

The 11th House represents friendship, networks, technology, social awareness, humanitarianism, and community. It is ruled by the planet Uranus. Celestial bodies moving across this house will allow you to reach a wider network of people and find your place within society. Technology has made it easier to keep in touch with friends and make new professional contacts, so take advantage of its benefits. Your support system is incredibly important, and you have a solid foundation for your relationships. If you ever find yourself dealing with serious problems, you know you have good people you can lean on.

12th House (Pisces): House of Unconscious

The 12th House represents the unconscious, spirituality, healing, karma, afterlife, esotericism, and the subconscious. It is ruled by the planet Neptune. When celestial bodies transit into this house, you will discover that some people need to be removed from your life. While you are empathetic and have no problem sharing your emotions with others, some bring too much toxicity and drama to them, which is something you shouldn't feel obligated to deal with. Remember that karma will always send back to you what you put into the world, so make sure you emit positivity wherever you go.

How to Read the Kabbalistic Natal Chart

Kabbalistic natal charts are generally depicted as a wheel broken up into slices, looking a bit like a pizza pie. The wheel usually has three concentric circles, breaking each slice into three sections. The outer circle shows the twelve zodiac signs, the middle circle shows the 10 astrological planets, and the innermost circle shows the twelve astrological house numbers. Some natal charts will use symbols for each circle, while others choose to depict the zodiac signs as date ranges instead, making it easier to find someone's birth date if they aren't familiar with the zodiac. Since not all sources give the exact same date ranges for each sign, this can also avoid any confusion when plotting out someone's natal chart.

Reading a natal chart involves charting the placement of the planets in the sky at the time of your birth, as well as your geographical location. This represents the different aspects of your personality, with each planet influencing a particular trait or characteristic about you. Certain planets also rule over different zodiac signs, which gives them a stronger connection to the attributes they possess. You will also need to find the ascendant in the natal chart. The ascendant the point that was rising over the eastern horizon at the precise moment you were born, measured by sign and degree. On the natal chart wheel, this can be found on the left side, at roughly the same place where 9:00 would be located on a clock. The descendant is on the opposite side at around the location of 3:00.

The first astrological house will always match up with the ascendant. The zodiac signs and astrological planets are placed around the wheel based on the first astrological house and the ascendant. Once you have set the zodiac signs and astrological planets into their correct positions based on the time and place of your birth, you can match them up and interpret their traits and characteristics like a horoscope. Depending on the orientation of the zodiac signs and astrological planets, you might have a stronger connection to certain attributes, personality types, behaviors, incarnations, and destinies. The planets represent your actions and motivations, the astrological houses express how you complete tasks in your life, and the zodiac signs depict the aspects of yourself that you can work on to grow and change.

Examples of Natal Chart Readings

Here are some examples of natal chart readings, using all the relevant information to determine the precise date, time, and location to get a comprehensive report on the example person's traits, characteristics, personality, and life goals:

Person A (Male): Born on September 17, 1993, at 6:48 AM in New York City, New York, USA

1st House (Ascendant): Virgo – Moon, Mercury, and Jupiter

2nd House: Libra – Mars

3rd House: Scorpio – Pluto and North Node

4th House: Sagittarius – Uranus and Neptune

5th House: Capricorn – Saturn

6th House: Aquarius

7th House (Descendant): Pisces

8th House: Aries

9th House: Taurus – South Node

10th House: Gemini

11th House: Cancer – Venus

12th House: Leo – Sun

Person A has a Virgo ascendant, and the Moon is also in Virgo. The North Node is in the 3rd House, and the Sun is in Leo and the 12th House. This means they are analytical, alert, social, intelligent, erudite, reserved, critical, helpful, and conscientious. They're the type of person who is a great public speaker but can put a bit too much pressure on others to live up to their standards. Likely career paths include politician, professor, lecturer, or social activist.

Person B (Female): Born on May 25, 1977, at 3:04 PM in Paris, France

1st House (Ascendant): Cancer

2nd House: Leo - Saturn

3rd House: Leo

4th House: Virgo - Pluto and North Node

5th House: Libra - Moon and Uranus

6th House: Sagittarius - Neptune

7th House (Descendant): Capricorn - Mercury and Mars

8th House: Aquarius - Sun

9th House: Aquarius

10th House: Pisces - Venus and South Node

11th House: Aries - Jupiter

12th House: Gemini

Person B has a Cancer ascendant. The North Node is in Virgo and the 4th House. The Moon is in the 5th House, and the Sun is in the 8th House. This means they are brave, independent, sensual, progressive, independent, and autonomous. They have an unusual, rebellious, and revolutionary spirit, as well as strong ideals and great courage in the face of adversity. Likely career paths include artist, social activist, journalist, or romance author.

Person C (Non-Binary): Born on June 26, 2001, at 10:31 PM in Tokyo, Japan

1st House (Ascendant): Pisces

2nd House: Aries - Venus

3rd House: Taurus - Saturn

4th House: Gemini - Sun, Mercury, Jupiter, and North Node

5th House: Cancer

6th House: Leo

7th House (Descendant): Virgo - Moon

8th House: Libra

9th House: Scorpio - Pluto

10th House: Sagittarius - Mars and South Node

11th House: Capricorn

12th House: Aquarius – Uranus and Neptune

Person C has a Pisces ascendant. The Sun and North Node are in Gemini and the 4th House. The Moon is in Virgo and the 7th House. This means they are tenacious, calm, tender, discreet, thoughtful, sensitive, humble, and impressionable. They have a strong sense of individuality, radiant, creative energy, very good memory, and strict emotional discipline. However, they can also be somewhat timid, indecisive, anxious, lazy, or manipulative. Likely, careers include scientist, doctor, surgeon, medical researcher, scholar, academic, or health care worker.

Chapter 9: Kabbalah and the Tarot Cards

The history of Kabbalah and Tarot are more closely intertwined than many people realize. While various sources give different dates of inception for Tarot, including Ancient Egypt, 13th century France, or 15th century Italy, one of the first definitive guides to Tarot was published by Kabbalist Eliphas Levi in 1856. The Dogme et Rituel de la Haute Magie (Dogma and Ritual of High Magic) was split into 22 chapters, mirroring the 22 cards of Tarot's Major Arcana. He also equated each Major Arcana card with a letter of the Hebrew alphabet and the four suits of the Minor Arcana with the Tetragrammaton.

In 1889, Levi's student, Gerard Encausse, published his own book focusing on Tarot under the name "Papus," titling it The Tarot of the Bohemians. Around the same time, the Swiss occultist Oswald Wirth put out the first deck of Major Arcana cards that incorporated the 22 Hebrew letters into their traditional designs. The Golden Dawn also utilized the Hebrew alphabet in their Tarot decks, even though they didn't print the letters on the cards themselves. Writings from members of the organization show that members assigned the sephirot to the ten numbered cards of the Minor Arcana and the Four Worlds to the four suits. Aleister Crowley even swapped the letters connected to the Major Arcana cards known as The Emperor and the Star, giving "Tsadi" to the Emperor and "He" to the Star.

Both Kabbalah and Tarot also share basic tenets in their belief systems. The four suits of the Tarot deck refer to different aspects of a person's life – the suit of Swords equates to knowledge, Wands to sexuality and passion, Cups to emotions, and Pentacles to money and careers. This correlates to the way the sephirot of the Tree of Life and Kabbalistic astrology express similar attributes when assigned to a person's life. The 22 cards of the Major Arcana have been equated with the 22 paths of the sephirot in the Tree of Life and the 22 letters of the Hebrew alphabet.

The Tarot Card System

The modern Kabbalistic Tarot card deck has 78 cards. There are 22 Major Arcana cards, each with its own name and associated traits, and 56 Minor Arcana cards. The Minor Arcana cards are divided into 4 suits, with 14 cards per suit. Each suit contains numbered cards, from 1 to 10, and 4 court cards, including the King, Queen, Knight, and Page. The 4 suits are named Swords, Wands, Cups, and Pentacles. Tarot cards can be used for cartomancy or the art of a special form of divination utilizing a deck of cards. In addition to fortune-telling, they can reveal all kinds of information that can help you find out more about yourself. This is referenced by the names of the two sets in the Tarot deck: Major Arcana means "greater secrets," and Minor Arcana means "lesser secrets."

Major Arcana Tarot Cards

The 22 Major Arcana Tarot cards are known as the named, numbered, or trump cards. They are generally assigned a standardized name and number combination, using Roman numerals for each one. However, the Fool card carries no number on its face, so the numerals only range from 1 to 21, rendered as I to XXI. Although the Fool can be placed at the top or the bottom of the set of named cards, unofficially giving it the number 0 (zero) or XXII (22), Kabbalistic Tarot decks usually assign it to the top and consider it numbered as 0.

Major arcana Tarot cards.
https://unsplash.com/photos/v3qrbAgm7q8

List of Cards

1. **The Fool (0):** Assigned the Hebrew letter Aleph. It is associated with the planet Uranus, the element of Air, and the zodiac sign of Aquarius. In different Tarot card systems, the Fool can either be placed first or last, but in Kabbalistic versions of the deck, it's always placed first. Although the card itself doesn't have a number on it, the Fool is considered the number zero when placed first or XXII (22) when placed last. This card depicts a man dressed in stereotypical foolish attire. When the card is upright, it represents adventure, innocence, and new beginnings. If it is reversed, it means recklessness, fearlessness, and taking unnecessary risks.

2. **The Magician (I):** Assigned the Hebrew letter Bet. It is associated with the planet Mercury, the element of Air, and the zodiac sign of Gemini. Typically, this card shows the figure of the Magician pointing upward with one hand and downwards with the other. This is taken to represent the phrase "as above, so below," often interpreted as meaning that whatever is created in the metaphysical realm will manifest in the physical world. The card also shows a table with a sword, wand, cup, and pentacle, which are the four suits of the Minor Arcana. When the card is upright, it represents willpower, creation, and manifestation. If it is reversed, it means manipulation, wasted talents, and a lack of foresight.

3. **The High Priestess (II):** Assigned the Hebrew letter Gimel. It is associated with the Moon, the element of Water, and the zodiac sign of Cancer. This card depicts a woman wearing blue robes in a seated position with her hands on her lap. There is a crescent moon at her feet, and she wears a horned crown on her head. She sits between a white pillar and a black pillar, which symbolizes duality. When the card is upright, it represents feminine divinity, intuition, and the unconscious. If it is reversed, it means silence, withdrawal, and repressed emotions.

4. **The Empress (III):** Assigned the Hebrew letter Dalet. It is associated with the planet Venus, the element of Fire, and the zodiac sign of Taurus. This card depicts a woman sitting on a throne and wearing a crown with twelve stars on top of it, symbolizing the twelve zodiac signs, twelve astrological houses, and twelve months of the year. She also holds a scepter in one hand, showing the power she holds over life. When the card is upright, it represents fertility, nourishment, abundance, and femininity. If it is reversed, it means emptiness, overbearing, and dependence.

5. **The Emperor (IV):** Assigned the Hebrew letter He (or Tsadi). It is associated with the planet Mars, the element of Fire, and the zodiac sign of Aries. This card depicts a regal-looking man sitting upon a throne adorned with ram heads. He wears a cloak and has a long, white beard, holding a scepter shaped like an Ankh in his right hand and a globe in his left hand. When the card is upright, it represents authority, structure, establishment, and paternal feelings. If it is reversed, it means inflexibility, domination, undisciplined, and excessive overt control.

6. **The Hierophant (V):** Assigned the Hebrew letter Vav. It is associated with the planet Venus, the element of Earth, and the zodiac sign of Taurus. This card depicts a religious leader holding his right hand aloft, with two fingers pointing up and two pointing down, symbolizing a bridge between Heaven and Hell. He has a triple cross-staff in his left hand and wears a triple-tiered crown. The Hierophant is positioned between two pillars, with one showing Obedience and the other Disobedience. When the card is upright, it represents tradition, ethics, morality, conformity, and spiritual wisdom. If it is reversed, it means subversiveness, freedom, rebellion, and personal beliefs.

7. **The Lovers (VI):** Assigned the Hebrew letter Zayin. It is associated with the planet Mercury, the element of Air, and the zodiac sign of Gemini. This card depicts a man and a woman (sometimes Adam and Eve) standing on opposite sides of an angelic figure looming overhead in the middle. When the card is upright, it represents love, harmony, partnerships, and decisions. If it is reversed, it means inequity, disharmony, powerlessness, and instability.

8. **The Chariot (VII):** Assigned the Hebrew letter Het. It is associated with the Moon, the element of Water, and the zodiac sign of Cancer. This card depicts a man in a chariot being pulled by a pair of horses or sphinxes, one colored black and the other white. He is wearing a crown or helmet and a set of stylized armor. The man is not holding any reins but is sometimes shown with a sword or wand in his hand. When upright, the card represents success, determination, control, direction, action, and strength of will. If it is reversed, it means opposition, inconsistency, and unreliability.

9. **Strength (VIII):** Assigned the Hebrew letter Tet. It is associated with the Sun, the element of Fire, and the zodiac sign of Leo. This card depicts a woman leaning over a lion, sometimes grabbing his jaws. Some versions show the infinity symbol above her head. When the card is upright, it represents strength, bravery, compassion, persuasiveness, focus, and influence. If it is reversed, it means weakness, insecurity, lethargy, and un-tempered emotions.

10. **The Hermit (IX):** Assigned the Hebrew letter Yod. It is associated with the planet Mercury, the element of Earth, and the zodiac sign of Virgo. This card is depicted as a cloaked and hooded old man standing atop a mountain. He has a staff in one hand and a lit lantern in the other, with the light coming from a six-pointed star. The light of the lantern symbolizes guidance into the unknown. When the card is upright, it represents solitude, wisdom, spiritual enlightenment, and passion. If it is reversed, it means loneliness, terror, anxiety, sadness, and depression.

11. **Wheel of Fortune (X):** Assigned the Hebrew letter Kaf. It is associated with the planet Jupiter, the element of Fire, and the zodiac sign of Capricorn. This card typically depicts a wheel or compass face, and it is sometimes inscribed with the letters T-A-R-O when reading clockwise from the top. There are usually figures,

animals, and other ornamentation surrounding the wheel. When upright, the card represents chance, destiny, fate, karma, turning points, and life cycles. If it is reversed, it means upheaval, unwanted change, obstacles, and being at the whim of outside forces.

12. **Justice (XI):** Assigned the Hebrew letter Lamed. It is associated with the planet Venus, the element of Air, and the zodiac sign of Libra. This card depicts a seated figure, such as a king or a judge, holding a sword in their right hand and a golden scale in their left hand. The scale symbolizes a fair and balanced decision. When the card is upright, it represents justice, integrity, legitimacy, rationality, civility, and life lessons. If it is reversed, it means injustice, fraud, irresponsibility, dishonesty, disloyalty, criminality, or acts of evil.

13. **The Hanged Man (XII):** Assigned the Hebrew letter Mem. It is associated with the planet Venus, the element of Earth, and the zodiac sign of Taurus. This card depicts a man hanging upside-down from a tree or the gallows, secured there by one foot. He is sometimes given a golden halo to symbolize martyrdom, atonement, or enlightenment. When the card is upright, it represents sacrifice, self-reflection, uncertainty, liberation, and spiritual development. If it is reversed, it means selfishness, stagnation, bad habits, and an unsolvable problem.

14. **Death (XIII):** Assigned the Hebrew letter, Nun. It is associated with the planet Pluto, the element of Water, and the zodiac sign of Scorpio. This card depicts the Grim Reaper wielding a scythe. He is sometimes shown wearing a suit of black armor and riding atop a pale horse. When upright, the card represents rebirth, transformation, modesty, powerful movement, simplification, and the end of a cycle. It means fear of new beginnings, restrictiveness, small-mindedness, and resistance to change if it is reversed.

15. **Temperance (XIV):** Assigned the Hebrew letter Samekh. It is associated with the planet Jupiter, the element of Fire, and the zodiac sign of Sagittarius. This card depicts a winged angel with a triangle inside a square on its chest. Just above these shapes is the Tetragrammaton. The angel has one foot on land and the other in water. When the card is upright, it represents balance, moderation, cooperation, and problem-solving. If it is reversed, it means

imbalance, discord, overindulgence, carelessness, and audacity.

16. **The Devil (XV):** Assigned the Hebrew letter Ayin. It is associated with the planet Saturn, the element of Earth, and the zodiac sign of Capricorn. This card depicts a large demonic figure on a pedestal with ram horns, bat wings, and the feet of a harpy. There is an upside-down pentagram on his forehead; his right hand is raised while his left is lowered and holding a torch. There is a pair of unclothed demons with tails, one of whom is male and the other female, both chained to the pedestal. When upright, the card represents betrayal, depression, addiction, captivity, negativity, and a focus on material things. It means freedom, independence, detachment, overcoming addiction, and a reclamation of power if it is reversed.

17. **The Tower (XVI):** Assigned the Hebrew letter Pe. It is associated with the planet Mars, the element of Fire, and the zodiac sign of Aries. This card depicts a large tower being struck by lightning and set ablaze while two people are either fleeing from an open door or leaping out of the flame-engulfed windows. When upright, the card represents release, tragedy, revelations, loss, and a sudden change. It means avoiding tragedy, resisting change, delaying the inevitable, and narrowly escaping danger if it is reversed.

18. **The Star (XVII):** Assigned the Hebrew letter Tsadi (or He). It is associated with the planet Uranus, the element of Air, and the zodiac sign of Aquarius. This card depicts an unclothed woman kneeling by the water, with one foot in the water and the other on land. She has a pair of jugs in her hands, pouring liquid into the water and onto the land. A large star is floating above her head, and seven smaller stars symbolizing the seven chakras are positioned around it. When the card is upright, it represents hope, recuperation, renewal, generosity, creativity, and inspiration. If it is reversed, it means despair, boredom, hopelessness, discouragement, and a lack of creativity or inspiration.

19. **The Moon (XVIII):** Assigned the Hebrew letter Qof. It is associated with the planet Neptune, the element of Water, and the zodiac sign of Pisces. This card depicts a scene at night where a wild wolf and a domesticated dog are both howling at the moon. The moon has sixteen larger rays and sixteen smaller rays, as well as fifteen dew drops falling from it. There are two pillars on

opposite sides of the card, and water near the bottom of the card with a crayfish emerging onto the land. When the card is upright, it represents confusion, fear, anxiety, delusion, and risk. If it is reversed, it means clarity, beating anxiety, overcoming fear, and uncovering the truth.

20. **The Sun (XIX):** Assigned the Hebrew letter, Resh. It is associated with the Sun, the element of Fire, and the zodiac sign of Leo. This card depicts an anthropomorphized sun with long rays being emitted from it and a row of sunflowers beneath it. There is a baby riding a white steed and holding a red banner or flag, symbolizing the blood of renewal. When the card is upright, it represents success, happiness, truth, fertility, and optimism. If it is reversed, it means failure, procrastination, sadness, and lies.

21. **Judgment (XX):** Assigned the Hebrew letter, Shin. It is associated with the planet Pluto and the element of Fire but has no corresponding zodiac sign. This card depicts a large, looming angel near the top who is blowing a trumpet with the flag of St. George hanging from it. The angel is sometimes said to be Metatron and a scene from the Book of Revelations. A group of ashy, sallow people is standing around, looking up at the angel with their arms extending toward him. They symbolize the resurrected emerging from their graves. When upright, the card represents rebirth, awakening, reflection, absolution, reckoning, and a spiritual calling. If it is reversed, it means uncertainty, insecurity, indecision, despondency, and melancholy.

22. **The World (XXI):** Assigned the Hebrew letter Tav. It is associated with the planet Saturn and the element of Earth but has no corresponding zodiac sign. This card depicts an unclothed woman dancing above the Earth. She is encircled by either a wreath or an ouroboros eating its own tail. There are figures in the four corners of the card – a man in the top left, an eagle in the top right, an ox in the bottom left, and a lion in the bottom right. When the card is upright, it represents unity, integration, fulfillment, completion, and a great journey. If it is reversed, it means emptiness, incompletion, shortcuts, delays, and confinement.

Kabbalistic Principles of Major Arcana Tarot Cards

In Kabbalah, the Major Arcana Tarot cards have a special esoteric significance. They are considered to be a "Bible of Bibles," capable of revealing every truth within all of creation. Since each named card of the Major Arcana has specific traits and characteristics associated with them, when performing a reading, they can unveil the secrets of a person's soul and uncover the mysteries of the past, present, and future. The archetypes depicted on each card represent the various forms of the world's human and divine aspects. There is a careful balance between the conscious and subconscious, the physical and metaphysical realms, positive and negative emotions, good and evil, and Man and God.

Connection to the 22 Paths

Kabbalah introduces a connection to the sephirot and the Tree of Life to the Major Arcana Tarot cards. Each named card is associated with a specific path along the Tree corresponding to its standard attributes. There are three distinct subsets of sephirotic paths within the Tree of Life: the column on the right is called the Pillar of Mercy, which embodies the positive, active, and male side. The column on the left is called the Pillar of Judgment and possesses the negative, passive, and female sides. The column in the middle is called the Pillar of Harmony, and it reconciles the two opposing sides by bringing them into balance.

The Major Arcana Tarot cards and their associated sephirot paths include:

1. **The Fool:** Keter to Chochmah (Pillar of Mercy)
2. **The Magician:** Keter to Binah (Pillar of Judgment)
3. **The High Priestess:** Keter to Tiferet (Pillar of Harmony)
4. **The Empress:** Chochmah to Binah (Pillar of Harmony)
5. **The Emperor:** Chochmah to Tiferet (Pillar of Mercy)
6. **The Hierophant:** Chochmah to Chesed (Pillar of Mercy)
7. **The Lovers:** Binah to Tiferet (Pillar of Judgment)
8. **The Chariot:** Binah to Geburah (Pillar of Judgment)
9. **Strength:** Chesed to Geburah (Pillar of Harmony)
10. **The Hermit:** Chesed to Tiferet (Pillar of Mercy)
11. **The Wheel of Fortune:** Chesed to Netsach (Pillar of Mercy)

12. **Justice:** Geburah to Tiferet (Pillar of Judgment)

13. **The Hanged Man:** Geburah to Hod (Pillar of Judgment)

14. **Death:** Tiferet to Netsach (Pillar of Mercy)

15. **Temperance:** Tiferet to Yesod (Pillar of Harmony)

16. **The Devil:** Hod to Tiferet (Pillar of Judgment)

17. **The Tower:** Netsach to Hod (Pillar of Harmony)

18. **The Star:** Yesod to Netsach (Pillar of Mercy)

19. **The Moon:** Netsach to Malkuth (Pillar of Mercy)

20. **The Sun:** Yesod to Hod (Pillar of Judgment)

21. **Judgment:** Hod to Malkuth (Pillar of Judgment)

22. **The World:** Malkuth to Yesod (Pillar of Harmony)

Minor Arcana Tarot Cards

The 56 Minor Arcana Tarot cards are the suit cards in a Tarot deck. They have 4 suits, each with cards numbered from 1 to 10. These cards are either unillustrated, only having pips denoting their number and suit, or will carry a thematically-consistent design. Some decks will use an Ace in place of the number 1, while others just use its actual number. There are also 4 court or face cards in each suit. These are generally given as King, Queen, Knight, and Page, but some versions will replace the Page with a Jack or Knave. The suits used are typically Swords, Wands, Cups, and Pentacles, but some decks will swap Swords with Blades or Spades; Wands with Staves, Clubs, or Batons; Cups with Chalices, Goblets, Hearts, or Vessels; and Pentacles with Coins, Rings, Diamonds, or Disks.

List of Cards

The suit of Swords represents actions, words, and thoughts:

1. **One (Ace) of Swords:** When upright, this card means triumph, conquest, and great prosperity. If reversed, it refers to hatred, failure, and great misery.

2. **Two of Swords:** When upright, this card means meditation, inner harmony, and balanced decisions. If reversed, it refers to blindness, fear, and rash decisions.

3. **Three of Swords:** When upright, this card means deep sorrow, lost relationships, and accidental death. If reversed, it refers to mitigated sorrow, missed connections, and premeditated murder.

4. **Four of Swords:** When upright, this card means vigilance, solitude, exile, coffin, and tomb. If reversed, it refers to precaution, avarice, testament, circumspection, economy, and wise administration.

5. **Five of Swords:** When upright, this card means confidence, potency, preparation, and victory. If reversed, it refers to the dangers of overconfidence or a victory that seems assured *turning into a defeat.*

6. **Six of Swords:** When upright, this card means movement, long journeys, escape from danger, fleeing from problems, relief from pain, and gradual change. If reversed, it refers to immobility, moving toward danger, endless pain, and sudden change.

7. **Seven of Swords:** When upright, this card means mind, intellect, and diplomacy over violence. If reversed, it refers to overthinking, surrender, and disinterest in solving a problem.

8. **Eight of Swords:** When upright, this card means impossible situations, sacrifice, and enduring pain to escape a trap. If reversed, it refers to the fear of acting, hesitancy to speak up, and acceptance of captivity.

9. **Nine of Swords:** When upright, this card means premonitions, deception, nightmares, depression, suffering, scandal, violence, disappointment, and cruelty. If reversed, it refers to unfounded fears, guilt, doubt, distrust, misery, malice, suspicion, imprisonment, and isolation.

10. **Ten of Swords:** When upright, this card means bleak situations, mental anguish, and temporary destruction. If reversed, it refers to long-term problems, finding the silver lining, and tempering despair to safeguard future opportunities for success.

11. **Page of Swords:** When upright, this card means curiosity, moving freely, and strong energy. If reversed, it refers to hindered movement, encumbrance, and indolence.

12. **Knight of Swords:** When upright, this card means foolish courage, clever liars, confident tricksters, and secrets. If reversed, it refers to reconsidering actions, avoiding mistakes, and remaining faithful.

13. **Queen of Swords:** When upright, this card means freedom of speech, unfiltered thoughts, active intelligence, and clarity of mind. If reversed, it refers to clouded thoughts, censorship, and dimwittedness.

14. **King of Swords:** When upright, this card means decisive, reasonable, understanding, and stout of heart. If reversed, it refers to ruthlessness, excessive judgment, and un-enlightenment.

The suit of Wands represents passion, motivation, and energy:

1. **One (Ace) of Wands:** When upright, this card means birth, ambition, creativity, good fortune, commencement, inventiveness, and new beginnings. If reversed, it refers to delayed progress, loss of wealth, illness, and greed.

2. **Two of Wands:** When upright, this card means achievement, boldness, partnership, and goals. If reversed, it refers to anxiety, doubt, meekness, and playing it safe.

3. **Three of Wands:** When upright, this card means long-term success, traveling, fresh starts, trade, and adventure. It refers to cessation, disappointment, toiling, and ending a task if reversed.

4. **Four of Wands:** When upright, this card means harmony, prosperity, celebrations, pleasure, and happiness. If reversed, it refers to transience, burdens, lack of support, conflict at home, and feeling unwelcome.

5. **Five of Wands:** When upright, this card means aggression, tension, conflict, rivalry, competition, arguments, and disagreement. It refers to cooperation, truce, peace, and resolving or avoiding conflict if reversed.

6. **Six of Wands:** When upright, this card means triumph, confidence, rewards, praise, recognition, acclaim, and pride. It refers to failure, feeling overlooked, financial loss, poor investments, and working without recognition if reversed.

7. **Seven of Wands:** When upright, this card means self-defense, protection, fighting for love, beating the odds, and undertaking a challenge. If reversed, it refers to yielding your ground, surrendering, defensiveness, losing a competition, or failure due to overconfidence.

8. **Eight of Wands:** When upright, this card means swiftness, snap decisions, excitement, speed, and progress. If reversed, it refers to misunderstanding, chaos, hastiness, waiting, unpreparedness, and sloth.

9. **Nine of Wands:** When upright, this card means persistence, perseverance, resilience, grit, fatigue, and last stands. If reversed, it

refers to defensiveness, stubbornness, rigidity, and a refusal to compromise.

10. **Ten of Wands:** When upright, this card means responsibility, duty, obligation, struggling, burdens, stress, and burning out. If reversed, it refers to breakdown, collapse, taking on too much responsibility, and inability to delegate.

11. **Page of Wands:** When upright, this card means excitement, cheerfulness, adventure, extroversion, energy, and new ideas. If reversed, it refers to impatience, tantrums, boredom, laziness, distractions, and unreliability.

12. **Knight of Wands:** When upright, this card means charm, rebellion, heroism, courage, energy, hot-tempered, and free spirits. If reversed, it refers to recklessness, arrogance, impatience, passivity, volatility, and domination.

13. **Queen of Wands:** When upright, this card means confidence, charisma, determination, optimism, self-assuredness, vivaciousness, and sociability. If reversed, it refers to vengeance, jealousy, temperamentality, demand, selfishness, timidity, and bullying.

14. **King of Wands:** When upright, this card means vision, leadership, boldness, taking control, and looking at the big picture. If reversed, it refers to tyranny, viciousness, powerlessness, forcefulness, ineffectiveness, and weakness.

The suit of Cups represents feelings, emotions, creativity, and intuition:

1. **One (Ace) of Cups:** When upright, this card means love, creativity, spirituality, emotional awakening, intuition, and new feelings. If reversed, it refers to emptiness, frigidity, gloominess, emotional loss, feeling unloved, and a creative block.

2. **Two of Cups:** When upright, this card means attraction, unity, mutual respect, partnership, connection, and forging close bonds. If reversed, it refers to rejection, imbalance, separation, tension, withdrawal, division, and poor communication.

3. **Three of Cups:** When upright, this card means community, friendship, gatherings, celebrations, social events, and group activities. If reversed, it refers to excessiveness, scandal, gossip, loneliness, isolation, solitude, and social imbalance.

4. **Four of Cups:** When upright, this card means apathy, melancholy, boredom, contemplation, discontentedness, indifference, and feeling disconnected. If reversed, it refers to awareness, negativity, clarity, acceptance, depression, and opting for happiness.

5. **Five of Cups:** When upright, this card means sadness, grief, loss, disappointment, mourning, and feeling discontent. If reversed, it refers to acceptance, contentment, moving on, positivity, and achieving inner peace.

6. **Six of Cups:** When upright, this card means nostalgia, sentimentality, familiarity, memories, comfort, healing, and pleasure. If reversed, it refers to independence, leaving home, moving forward, and being stuck in the past.

7. **Seven of Cups:** When upright, this card means illusion, daydreams, fantasy, choices, wishful thinking, indecision, and seeking a purpose. If reversed, it refers to distraction, diversion, disarray, clarity, feeling adrift, and making a choice.

8. **Eight of Cups:** When upright, this card means seeking truth, abandonment, letting go, escapism, and choosing happiness over money. If reversed, it refers to stagnation, avoidance, monotony, fearing change, acceptance of loss, and remaining in a bad situation.

9. **Nine of Cups:** When upright, this card means contentment, success, recognition, satisfaction, achievement, pleasure, and wish fulfillment. If reversed, it refers to disappointment, unhappiness, arrogance, underachievement, snobbery, and lacking fulfillment.

10. **Ten of Cups:** When upright, this card means homecoming, security, happiness, emotional stability, and domestic harmony. If reversed, it refers to separation, disharmony, isolation, and domestic conflict.

11. **Page of Cups:** When upright, this card means sensitivity, naivete, idealism, innocence, a dreamer, and one's inner child. If reversed, it refers to immaturity, insecurity, escapism, emotional vulnerability, and neglecting your inner child.

12. **Knight of Cups:** When upright, this card means charm, artistry, gracefulness, idealism, tactfulness, diplomacy, mediation, and negotiation. If reversed, it refers to moodiness, disappointment, turmoil, vanity, throwing tantrums, and avoiding conflict.

13. **Queen of Cups:** When upright, this card means warmth, compassion, kindness, supportiveness, intuition, counseling, and healing. If reversed, it refers to insecurity, neediness, fragility, martyrdom, dependence, oversharing, and excessively sensitive.

14. **King of Cups:** When upright, this card means wisdom, diplomacy, advisor, devotion, and striking a balance between your head and heart. If reversed, it refers to anxiety, coldness, repression, withdrawal, manipulation, selfishness, and feeling overwhelmed.

The suit of Pentacles represents work, finances, and material possessions:

1. **One (Ace) of Pentacles:** When upright, this card means resourcefulness, abundance, security, prosperity, stability, manifestation, and new opportunities. If reversed, it refers to scarcity, instability, deficiency, stinginess, missed chances, and poor investments.

2. **Two of Pentacles:** When upright, this card means adaptation, flexibility, resourcefulness, and balancing or stretching resources. If reversed, it refers to disorganization, imbalance, messiness, chaos, overextension, and feeling overwhelmed.

3. **Three of Pentacles:** When upright, this card means teamwork, collaboration, effort, apprenticeship, combined goals, and shared energy. If reversed, it refers to apathy, conflict, egotism, idleness, competition, disunity, and lacking cohesion.

4. **Four of Pentacles:** When upright, this card means possessiveness, stinginess, hoarding, security, materialism, savings, frugality, accumulated wealth, boundaries, and guardedness. If reversed, it refers to generosity, recklessness, insecurity, reckless spending, vulnerability, and financial mismanagement.

5. **Five of Pentacles:** When upright, this card means hardship, loss, adversity, isolation, disgrace, alienation, unemployment, struggles, and feeling abandoned. If reversed, it refers to forgiveness, overcoming adversity, recovering from loss, positive changes, and welcomeness.

6. **Six of Pentacles:** When upright, this card means charity, community, support, gratitude, sharing, generosity, and transactions. If reversed, it refers to inequity, extortion, abusing generosity, power dynamics, and gifts with strings attached.

7. **Seven of Pentacles:** When upright, this card means progress, growth, rewards, harvest, results, perseverance, planning, and patience. If reversed, it refers to waste, setbacks, impatience, procrastination, stagnation, lack of effort, unfinished work, or unrewarded effort.

8. **Eight of Pentacles:** When upright, this card means craftsmanship, skill, talent, quality, expertise, mastery, dedication, accomplishment, commitment, and high standards. If reversed, it refers to laziness, ill-repute, poor quality, unskilled, demotivation, and being stuck in a dead-end job.

9. **Nine of Pentacles:** When upright, this card means success, independence, achievement, leisure, self-sufficiency, financial security, and rewarded efforts. If reversed, it refers to reckless spending, superficiality, financial instability, guardedness, and living beyond your means.

10. **Ten of Pentacles:** When upright, this card means ancestry, legacy, family, roots, inheritance, foundation, privilege, affluence, tradition, and stability. If reversed, it refers to bankruptcy, debt, instability, familial disputes, financial conflict, and breaking tradition.

11. **Page of Pentacles:** When upright, this card means ambition, diligence, planning, consistency, studiousness, loyalty, faithfulness, dependability, and groundedness. If reversed, it refers to foolishness, immaturity, irresponsibility, procrastination, laziness, underachievement, and missed chances.

12. **Knight of Pentacles:** When upright, this card means practicality, efficiency, reliability, commitment, patience, reliability, conservative, and steadfastness. If reversed, it refers to boredom, irresponsibility, gambling, indifference, and being a workaholic.

13. **Queen of Pentacles:** When upright, this card means nurturing, caring, sensibility, practicality, welcoming, luxuriousness, being a homebody, and a good head for business. If reversed, it refers to selfishness, jealousy, insecurity, greed, unkemptness, materialism, intolerance, envy, self-absorption, and shallowness.

14. **King of Pentacles:** When upright, this card means prosperity, ambition, abundance, safety, kindness, protectiveness, providing sensuality, reliability, security, business acumen, and patriarchy. If reversed, it refers to materialism, greed, wastefulness,

exploitativeness, possessiveness, chauvinism, and poor investments.

Kabbalistic Principles of Minor Arcana Tarot Cards

In Kabbalah, the Minor Arcana Tarot cards represent the more mundane aspects of your life. The court cards symbolize the types of people you will meet on a day-to-day basis. Swords embody nobles and military personnel, Wands depict artisans and craftsmen, Cups reference the clergy, and Pentacles show merchants, vendors, and traders. The ten numbered cards can also be equated with the ten sephirot in the Tree of Life and their primary attributes. This includes:

- **Ones (Aces):** Keter – Crown (Point)
- **Twos:** Chochmah – Wisdom (Force)
- **Threes:** Binah – Understanding (Form)
- **Fours:** Chesed – Love or Mercy (Expanding)
- **Fives:** Geburah – Strength (Organizing)
- **Sixes:** Tiferet – Beauty (Awareness)
- **Sevens:** Netsach – Victory (Emotions)
- **Eights:** Hod – Glory (The Mind)
- **Nines:** Yesod – Foundation (The Psyche)
- **Tens:** Malkuth – Kingdom (Activity)

The Four Suits and the Kabbalistic Worlds

Each Minor Arcana suit corresponds to the Four Worlds from the Kabbalistic Tree of Life. They also have a connection to different aspects of the metaphysical realms and facets of life. These include:

- **Swords:** Yetzirah – Formation (Thinking)
- **Wands:** Atziluth – Emanation (Spirit)
- **Cups:** Beriah – Creation (Feeling)
- **Pentacles:** Assiah – Action (Doing)

Kabbalah delves into the secrets of the hidden world, and the correlation between the Minor Arcana suits and the Four Worlds, combined with the numbered cards and sephirot, are expressed through specific verses and keywords by using the prompts of "Life is..." or

"Creation is..." For example:

- The Four of Swords would be associated with the sephirah of Chesed and the world of Yetzirah. Translated through the corresponding attributes, this would be rendered as "Life is expanding your thinking." This can be adjusted to read, "Life is a growth of your mindset."

- The Ten of Pentacles is associated with the sephirah of Malkuth and the world of Assiah. It would be rendered as "Creation is the activity of doing," or when adjusted, it becomes "Creation is the act of doing."

- The Seven Cups are associated with Netsach and Beriah. It would be rendered as "Life is emotions you are feeling" or "Life is experiencing the gamut of emotions."

- The Six Wands are associated with Tiferet and Atziluth. This is rendered as "Life is an awareness of your spirit" or "Life has a spiritual awakening."

Tarot and the Tetragrammaton

The Tetragrammaton, or the four Hebrew letters that make up the name of God, can be associated with the four suits in the Minor Arcana. Since each card in the Major Arcana is assigned a Hebrew letter, they also correspond to the Tetragrammaton. It is usually rendered as Yod-He-Vav-He (יהוה). Those who can learn how to properly pronounce this name are said to possess the power to release all hidden and arcane knowledge in the universe.

When connecting the Tetragrammaton to the Minor Arcana, you need to look at the numerical values of each Hebrew letter: Yod is 10, He is 5, and Vav is 6.

Therefore, the cards chosen to represent it would be:

the 10 of Swords,

5 of Wands,

6 of Cups,

5 of Pentacles

Rendered using the sephirot and Four Worlds combinations, it would be:

Malkuth and Yetzirah

Geburah and Atziluth

Tiferet and Beriah

Geburah and Assiah

Taking the Major Arcana cards related to the Tetragrammaton, you would have the Hermit for Yod, the Emperor for He, the Hierophant for Vav, and the Emperor for He again. These can be combined with the Four Worlds, just like the Minor Arcana cards, or they can be taken alone, looking at the associated paths along the Tree of Life. Interestingly, they all involve the same three sephirot: Chochmah, Chesed, and Tiferet. The Hermit is paired with Chesed to Tiferet, the Emperor with Chochmah to Tiferet, and the Hierophant with Chochmah to Chesed.

When looking at a diagram of the Tree of Light, you can see that these three paths create the shape of an irregular triangle in the upper right portion. Three is a sacred number in Kabbalah, just as it is in Judaism, Islam, and Christianity. There are three parts to the Torah, three patriarchs, and three angels visited Abraham, and the Jewish people are meant to pray three times a day. The twelve tribes of Israel were arrayed into four equal groups consisting of three tribes each when around the Tabernacle. This reflects how the Tetragrammaton uses three individual Hebrew letters in a set of four to spell out the name of God.

Chapter 10: Qabalistic Tarot Reading

Now that you understand the individual cards of the Tarot deck and what they represent, it's time to learn how to actually perform a reading with them. Readings are the method used to uncover the secrets about yourself and your life, making them a key component of Kabbalah and Tarot. Without knowing how to properly perform a reading, everything else concerning a Tarot deck is effectively useless. This is something that requires plenty of practice – nobody gets it exactly right on their first try, so don't feel discouraged if it takes time before you start to get the hang of it. Performing a truly comprehensive reading involves years of careful study to master, but you can learn how to do a relatively basic reading far quicker than that.

It takes practice and focus to be able to read the Tarots properly.
https://unsplash.com/photos/Ka-speuU7W4

Preparing a Reading

Making the right preparations before attempting a reading is necessary to ensure success. If you don't follow these steps, it will throw off the entire process, leaving any results open to error and misinterpretation. The main thing you need to remember is to always stay focused. Don't let your attention wander because while preparing your deck, there will be a connection between your mind, body, and spirit. Even your emotional state can influence a reading, so try to remain calm and collected as you prepare.

Choose Your Deck

The first thing you must do is choose your deck. Make sure it has all 78 cards with the right Major and Minor Arcana cards, as laid out in the previous chapter. A popular choice for Kabbalists is the Rider-Waite deck, which features the correct setup and has iconic artwork most often associated with Tarot. Your decision here is important since which specific cards you have in your deck will determine the traits and characteristics available when performing a reading.

Shuffle the Cards

After you have your chosen Tarot cards deck, you must shuffle them thoroughly. However, this isn't the same as shuffling playing cards. While shuffling, you must meditate on the areas of your life where you seek more clarity. This is part of the mystical aspect of Tarot reading. By thinking about the answers, you want, you will emit that energy using the deck as a conduit and manifest the results by imbuing each card with that metaphysical energy. You also need to decide if you want to include reversed cards. These have different meanings associated with them, and if you would like to include them, you need to alter the manner in which you shuffle the deck to randomize the orientation of each card by turning some 180 degrees.

Clear and Reset the Deck

If you've used the Tarot deck to perform a reading before, you need to clear and reset them. This involves reshuffling at least once but usually will take multiple shuffles to get right. The objective is to remove any residual energy from your previous reading, as having "tainted" cards will negatively impact your next attempt. An easy way to ensure your cards have been cleared and reset to neutral means cutting the deck into three parts, shuffling each one individually, and then recombining them for one final shuffle.

Pick a Spread

In Tarot readings, a spread is a structure you use when searching for the answers to whatever you wish to learn. Each of the positions where you lay the cards reflects a particular aspect of your queries. There are relatively simple spreads that will utilize fewer cards, making them easy for beginners to pick up. However, the amount of detail and depth in a reading is dependent on how many cards are in your spread. The more cards you use, the more comprehensive your answers will be, but this also requires more practice and focus on accomplishing.

Performing a Three Card Spread

If you're just starting out reading Tarot cards, it's best to begin slowly. For your first attempt, try doing what is known as a Three Card Spread. Its structure is easy enough to understand since it only uses three cards. The two most common configurations involve them representing either the past, present, and future or the self, path, and potential. Consider what question you want to be answered and focus on it. Think about the intricacies of what you're asking, and speak it out loud if it helps you to visualize it. Once you have made your intentions known, all you need to do is set your shuffled deck face-down on a surface and draw a card from the top. Going from left to right, place three cards in a horizontal row.

With the first configuration, the leftmost card is the past, the middle card is the present, and the rightmost card is the future. Using the second configuration, the left will be the self, the middle will be the path, and the right will be the potential. After you have placed all three cards, ruminate on what they mean using your first impression and intuition. You will still look up their proper meanings later, but it's good to check your gut reaction. Sometimes, your unconscious mind will pick up on something you haven't realized. Think about how each card makes you feel based on their names, numbers, and artwork. Just remember that everything is not what it seems – a meaning that may seem obvious on the surface can represent something very different once you analyze it with the proper information.

Following your first impressions, refer to the lists in previous chapters to find what your cards really represent. Remember the significance of each card's placement since their traits and characteristics will inform how they're interpreted based on whether the card is revealing something about the past, present, or future. Alternatively, reflect on how the meaning can be altered depending on whether they connect to the self, path, or potential. Since you're only using a Three Card Spread, you won't have to make sense of too much information. Still, interpreting the meaning of your cards can take a few times to figure out, so be ready to try a second or third attempt before you become more comfortable with performing a reading.

Examples of a Three Card Spread Reading

In a Three Card Spread using the first configuration, if you get the Fool in the Past, the Two of Cups in the Present, and the Moon in the Future, when asking the question, "Should I ask my partner to marry me?":

- **Past:** You were open to new possible relationships and didn't stick to conventional titles or gender roles. You learned through trial and error in past relationships what you want in a spouse and what it takes to keep it healthy. You entered relationships with trust and enthusiasm but had unrealistic expectations. There wasn't much planning for the future, and the course your relationships took may have appeared foolish to others. However, even after being hurt in the past, you refused to let that hold you back and were willing to open your heart to someone new.

- **Present:** Opposites attract, and there may just be plenty of magnetism in your current relationship. You have done the dance of courtship, entwined your energies together, and felt the sparks between you both. The emotional bonds forged occurred naturally, and both of you seem to complement each other in behavior and temperament while also sharing plenty of interests in which you are of one mind. Your relationship has great affection, and as kindred spirits, an engagement or marriage is on the horizon.

- **Future:** You are creative, intuitive, and empathetic. Things in your relationship might become intense, but you need to control your emotions. There is a risk of allowing your imagination to run wild, making you paranoid and hysterical when something triggers memories of failed relationships in the past. You or your partner will suffer from extreme mood swings and become almost as unfamiliar as total strangers. Find a way to conquer your fear and temper your imagination. Use the light of reason to lead you away from the shadows of deception and despair.

In a Three Card Spread using the second configuration, if you get the Hermit in Self, the Nine of Pentacles in Situation, and the Nine of Cups in Challenges, when asking the question, "Will I get a job as an actor?":

- **The Self:** Think deeply about why you wish to become an actor. What facet of the profession are you most drawn toward? You might love telling stories through a visual medium, using your body language, facial expressions, and manner of speech to convey meaning to the audience. Maybe you wish to be rich and famous, so you view acting as a way to get there. However, being an actor can be a lonely existence. You may connect on a deep level with those who watch you, but a screen or stage separates you from them. Adoring fans will seek you out, but they cannot relate to you or to your reality. Other actors face the same issues, but it isn't always easy to forge lasting bonds when the people you work with are constantly changing. Consider whether this is something you can handle and if the result is worth the sacrifice.

- **The Path:** Reaching the level of fame you seek as an actor comes with a price. Early on, you may struggle, lacking a stable paycheck. Until you can become financially independent, you will have to rely on taking other jobs with flexible schedules to accommodate the audition process, or you will need someone else to subsidize your financial responsibilities. Once you reach your goal, you will find money in abundance and have every luxury available. Becoming self-sufficient will create a sense of satisfaction, especially if you lack financial independence before achieving your dream.

- **The Potential:** Becoming an actor will satisfy you. There will be great contentment in getting to do what you love as a career. You will have plenty of gratitude for all those who helped you succeed, and you will want to do whatever you can to repay their kindness. However, avoid the pitfalls of professional and financial prosperity. It's all too easy to let an enjoyment of luxury transform into greed and materialism. Overindulging in anything that brings you happiness can cause it to suddenly taste sour. Finding inner peace will help center you and prevent you from falling too far off the path. Remember this, and you will always know how to find your way back again.

The Kabbalistic Tree of Life Tarot Spread

The Kabbalistic Tree of Life Tarot Spread involves structuring the cards in the same positions as the sephirot on the Tree of Life. Starting at the top in the Keter position, you will lay the cards out, moving from right to left. It will look something like this:

- First card at the top in the middle, standing in for Keter
- Second card down and to the right from the first, standing in for Chochmah
- Third card on the opposite side of the Tree from the second, standing in for Binah
- Fourth card beneath the second card, standing in for Chesed
- Fifth card beneath the third card, standing in for Geburah
- Sixth card down and to the left of the fourth card or down and to the right of the fifth card, standing in for Tiferet
- Seventh card beneath the fourth card, standing in for Netsach
- Eighth card beneath the fifth card, standing in for Hod
- Ninth card beneath the sixth card, standing in for Yesod
- Tenth card beneath the ninth card, standing in for Malkuth

Each position in the Tree of Life Spread is associated with a particular trait. These connect to ten of the twelve astrological houses, with two being combined with similar houses to fit the ten-card structure. The list of which houses belong to which card includes:

- **First Card:** Self
- **Second Card:** Social Status
- **Third Card:** Unconscious
- **Fourth Card:** Home and Family
- **Fifth Card:** Partnerships and Friendships
- **Sixth Card:** Possessions
- **Seventh Card:** Communication
- **Eighth Card:** Philosophy
- **Ninth Card:** Health and Pleasure
- **Tenth Card:** Transformation

Examples of a Tree of Life Spread Reading
Example #1

Here is an example of reading for a Tree of Life Spread when asking the question, "Should I hire my nephew for a job opening at my company, even though he's not the most qualified candidate?":

- **First Card:** Page of Swords
- **Second Card:** King of Swords
- **Third Card:** Knight of Cups
- **Fourth Card:** Three of Wands
- **Fifth Card:** Nine of Swords
- **Sixth Card:** Ace of Pentacles
- **Seventh Card:** Seven of Wands
- **Eighth Card:** Three of Swords
- **Ninth Card:** King of Cups
- **Tenth Card:** The Wheel of Fortune

First Card: You need to be decisive with your choice. This is a time of positive change in your life. Don't weigh yourself down by making a decision that will come back to haunt you.

Second Card: You need to make your decision without prejudice. Do not be swayed by favoritism or nepotism. Hiring someone based on external pressure or outside influences is not a good idea.

Third Card: It's time for creativity and passion for meeting action. The person you hire should be equally as eager to do this job. While you may feel a sense of benevolence by helping your nephew, you may find yourself wishing you had gone with a better candidate if he cannot perform up to your expectations.

Fourth Card: Plans for the open position at work are already moving forward. Whoever is hired needs to be able to hit the ground running. There will be plenty of opportunities for the new employee to prove himself, but it will only be successful if you insert the correct piece into the plans.

Fifth Card: You are going to experience a lot of stress from your decision. No matter what you do, somebody is going to miss out on a great opportunity. If you hire your nephew, your family will be happy, but you're also putting your professional reputation on the line. Should he fail to meet expectations, the anger and frustration will fall on you. However, if you hire somebody else, your nephew and your family are going to be furious with you. There will be serious tension during any get-togethers, and it will be seen as you betraying them.

Sixth Card: There will be a new and unexpected opportunity for you in this process. Success in hiring the right candidate will lead to a clear path for these opportunities. However, you must first take the proper steps to achieve it. This opportunity may not be immediately obvious, but you should trust that the hidden path will reveal itself when the time comes.

Seventh Card: You will have to take on an aggressive posture to stand up to injustice. There might be plenty of pressure on you to hire your nephew, but you know it would be wrong when there are better candidates out there. Be firm in your decision, no matter what trouble comes your way.

Eighth Card: There is going to be a great deal of sadness and heartbreak in the near future. Differences between you and your family will not easily be reconciled. They will feel bad if you don't hire your nephew, and this dispute will become a painful separation. Contemplate this loss and consider what mistakes could have been made, such as introducing the job opening to your nephew in the first place.

Ninth Card: You are a mentor, teacher, and father figure. There is great maturity and personal strength within you, which draws people to you. One of the things they gravitate toward is your ability to lead by example. Show others that you will make the right decision, even when it isn't easy. Although your paternal relationship with your nephew may be threatened, you will likely find yourself taking up this role with the candidate you hire.

Tenth Card: Fate has a tendency to spin off in new directions. New opportunities will present themselves, and there will be something unexpected in the near future. Be open to the new doors fate unlocks for you. Get ready to seize the day.

Example #2

Here is an example of reading for a Tree of Life Spread when asking the question, "Why is it so hard for me to make friends?":

- **First Card:** Temperance
- **Second Card:** Seven of Wands
- **Third Card:** Six of Swords
- **Fourth Card:** Strength

- **Fifth Card:** Nine of Swords
- **Sixth Card:** Six of Cups
- **Seventh Card:** Queen of Cups
- **Eighth Card:** Four of Wands
- **Ninth Card:** Three of Swords
- **Tenth Card:** Three of Cups

First Card: Moderation is important in all aspects of your life, including the physical, spiritual, intellectual, and emotional facets. Try to walk a middle road, finding a balance between everything. Don't be too overly eager to befriend someone. People can sense when you're trying too hard, and it puts them off. Finding commonalities with others can help you make connections, but don't pursue friendships where it only satisfies one aspect of your life. When you connect with someone in all areas, the bonds forged will remain stronger since you have more in common than if you only had an intellectual connection or a spiritual one.

Second Card: You are someone who stands up to injustice and refuses to back down, no matter how many people tell you to give up. This can sometimes alienate people, but anyone who is willing to accept unfair treatment or attitudes is not the type of person you want as a friend. Don't forget that it doesn't matter how many friends you have; what matters is the quality of the few friends in your life.

Third Card: Like many people, you carry a fair amount of emotional baggage. You might have been betrayed or lied to by friends in the past, and this has prevented you from making genuine connections with the people you meet. There is a place for bad memories and regret, but you need to transform into someone who has hope for what lies ahead. Instead of thinking about how many friends you've lost, look forward to the ones you will make in the future.

Fourth Card: You are someone with a great amount of power. This doesn't necessarily mean you wield power but that you possess a lot of inner strength. You have a strong personal character, and you don't waver on upholding your values. Try to channel this strength and determination into working on your social life. Rejection can be scary, but it's okay that not everyone will like you. There is somebody out there who will connect with you on a deeper level because of your inner fortitude. Remember: lots of people like to eat candy, but not everyone likes to eat candy. That doesn't mean there's anything wrong with candy - you just might need to sift through those who don't to find one that does.

Fifth Card: Your lack of a social life causes you a great deal of stress and anxiety. This has become a self-fulfilling prophecy for you. You are nervous and anxious about meeting new people, so when you meet new people, you act nervous and anxious. This turns them off to the idea of befriending you, which further isolates you and adds to your stress and anxiety. It has snowballed out of control, but once you have recognized that the fear is self-generated, you can take steps to break free from its control.

Sixth Card: Surround yourself with positivity and think positive thoughts. This will put out positive energy, to which people are bound to respond. Friendships can bring both parties much happiness, and the more you share good times with them, the more positive memories you will make. This will reinforce your friendships and help you stay friends for a long time.

Seventh Card: You are someone who is calm, supportive, and trustworthy. These are great traits to have in a friend. If you continue to support others and prove you are someone they can rely on, the strength of your friendship will only increase. Compassion can go a long way to make someone interested in befriending you. There are plenty of people out there who possess the same kinds of traits, and they may just be in need of a good friend, too.

Eighth Card: There will soon be a homecoming of an old circle of your friends. This is a chance to reconnect with those people you lost touch with or reignite a friendship that has been neglected. You can find comfort in familiar faces, and that leads to more happiness. It's also possible that in reconnecting with an old friend, you will find a new one among their own current social circle.

Ninth Card: Sometimes, people grow apart. As the differences in your goals and values become more pronounced, you may simply be too incompatible anymore. It's okay to mourn the loss of a friendship, but don't spend an excessive amount of time pining for the past. There are new people to meet and adventures to be had, and there's no need for bitterness over the end of an old friendship.

Tenth Card: Good friendships include open and honest communication between both parties. Don't hesitate to tell someone about your goals, fears, hopes, and dreams. You should celebrate your friendships, both past and present, because they helped shape you into the person you are today. Even friendships that turned sour contributed to the wonderful human being you have become, so be thankful for them as well. Feel free to express yourself, and there will be someone who relates to your thoughts and ideas. This plants the seed for a friendship to blossom in the future.

Conclusion

The benefits of Kabbalah and Astrology on the spiritual development of your soul cannot be overstated. There is a reason why they've withstood the test of time. What you can learn about yourself is immense, and those who have practiced Kabbalah and Astrology can attest to its applicability in real life. The steady march of science and technology is a wonderful thing, but there will always be room for religion, esotericism, and mysticism in this world. Too much remains unexplained and undiscovered to claim they have no place in modern society.

It's a sad truth that not everybody will respect your beliefs, but that doesn't mean you should give them up. There are more than enough people who share your enthusiasm for things like Kabbalah and Astrology to foster a healthy-sized community. Be proud of the person you are and the convictions you hold. What you've learned throughout this book should only reinforce those beliefs, as you've seen just how far-reaching Kabbalah and Astrology really are. They have such a rich history that it would be folly to presume every single person across thousands of years who has practiced these disciplines was wasting their time and energy on something that didn't yield results.

All the connections between Kabbalah, Astrology, and Tarot prove that there is something more to them than meets the eye. The way things like the Hebrew alphabet, the sephirot, the Tree of Life, the signs of the zodiac, the astrological planets, and both the Major and Minor Arcana of a Tarot card deck seem to intermingle is akin to symbiotic life forms in a natural ecosystem. They feed off one another and enhance the meaning behind each of them, generating a perpetual cycle of life, just as God is described as "the beginning and the end" while creating everything in between, the interactions and associations within each aspect of Kabbalah, Astrology, and Tarot are constantly finding new minds to make new connections.

There isn't a downside to learning more about Kabbalah and Astrology. It doesn't matter whether you only have a passing interest in it or if you intend to completely immerse yourself in your studies, absorbing as much about them as possible. You can take the information provided to you and use it as a stepping stone to greater knowledge and understanding. By diving into the mysteries of the universe, you can reveal the secrets about yourself that you weren't even aware were hiding deep down inside you. Let this book continue to guide you along your journey into Kabbalah and Astrology.

Part 2: Tarot for Beginners

What You Need to Know about Reading Tarot Cards, Spreads, Astrology, Kabbalah, Divination, Psychic Development, and Numerology

Introduction

The Tarot is a map of human consciousness encompassing your life's journey. Tarot card reading is the art and practice of divining wisdom and knowledge from a tarot card deck. The cards provide in-depth insights into your problems and can be used to seek solutions to these problems. The cards do not foretell anything but simply help you delve deep into your consciousness to find answers that are already embedded there.

This book combines the power of tarot cards with the esoteric knowledge of Kabbalah, the energy of numbers, and the secrets of astrology. Combining the limitless power of these divination tools, you can read tarot cards with great accuracy and find solutions and answers to questions for yourself and other's seeking a reading, referred to as querents.

The best thing about this book is that it speaks to novice and experienced readers alike. It is excellent for beginners as the basics are explained in simple, easy-to-understand language. It contains hands-on methods and instructions that you can practice daily to become an effective tarot card reader.

Tarot card reading by itself is a great tool, but when you combine it with the insights given by Kabbalistic, astrological, and numerological divination tools, then the outcome can be significantly better. This book teaches you the basics of the other three divination tools. It explains how they can be combined with the energy of a tarot card deck to get amazing results.

So, go on, turn the page, and discover the power of tarot card reading.

Chapter 1: Tarot Basics

At first glance, a dark Tarot deck may seem just like any other deck of playing cards. Well, nothing could be further from the truth. Tarot cards have been used for self-discovery, divination, and other magical, mystical purposes.

Tarot cards have been used for centuries.
https://pixabay.com/es/photos/artesan%c3%ada-tarot-adivinaci%c3%b3n-2728227/

History of Tarot Cards

The Tarot's magical calling has attracted a lot of magic practitioners for centuries. It is one of the most common divination tools humans have used for a long time. The history of tarot cards can be traced back to the 14th century in Europe. European artists are credited with creating the first tarot cards used for games only. These European artists created four suits similar to the ones in use today.

The Italians invented the tarot card deck in the 1430s. Artists added a fifth suit of 21 cards to the existing 4-suit playing card deck. The 21 newly-added, specially-designed cards were called Trionfi, Tarocchi, or "triumph." Another odd card called il Matto, or "the Fool," was also added to make the tarot deck a collection of 78 cards. Tarot cards were commonly used in Venice, Milan, Florence, and Urbino.

With the growing popularity of tarot card decks, rich Italian families such as the Visconti family of Milan began ordering customized decks to include paintings and portraits of their close friends and family members. The Italian artists created customized trump (or triumph) cards for these wealthy families.

This was an expensive affair and was restricted to the rich. One luxury tarot deck that survived from the mid-15th century is believed to have been customized for Filippo Maria Visconti, the last duke of Milan. However, with the advent of the printing press, tarot cards became more affordable, and even common citizens could enjoy using them in their homes.

Until the 16th century, tarot cards were used only to play games, especially popular in France and Italy. From around the 16th and 17th centuries, the Tarot also picked up pace as a divination tool. Yet, it was not until the 18th century that the meanings for each specific card were concretized, and layouts and spreads began to be formed.

In 1781, Antoine Court de Gebelin wrote a detailed analysis of the tarot card decks and the specific meanings and symbolism of each card. Further, he connected the symbolism and meaning to occult knowledge of ancient Egypt, especially with the legends of Egyptian gods such as Isis and Osiris. This work became very popular among the rich Europeans seeking esoteric knowledge.

Jean-Baptiste Alliette, a French occultist, countered Gebelin's work with his own theories and ideas a few years later. In his book, Alliette explained how to use the tarot card deck as a divination tool. Also, in 1791, he designed the first tarot card deck specifically created for divination rather than for playing purposes.

Divination and occult studies became very popular among rich Europeans during and after the Victorian Era. Events of the occult, such as seances and tarot card readings, were common at parties and social gatherings. Today, tarot card readings are among the most commonly used divination tools.

The Structure of a Tarot Card Deck

A Tarot card deck comprises 78 cards divided into two groups: the Major Arcana and Minor Arcana. The word Arcana is rooted in "arcane," which is, in turn, rooted in the Latin word "Arcanum," which translates to "secret or mysterious" or "something that is known or understood by very few people."

The Major Arcana, also called Trumps, consists of 22 cards and starts with Fool's card, or the Zero (0) card. The rest of them have the numbers 1 to 21 on them. Each of the 22 cards signifies a specific esoteric meaning. The Major Arcana depicts the soul's journey (represented by the Fool) as it passes through various stages of self-awareness and knowledge until it reaches possible enlightenment. The Major Arcana represent the archetypal elements people see and interact with in the world. Each archetype signifies a crucial stage of spiritual and/or psychological development.

The Minor Arcana, also called Pips, consists of 56 cards representing the "minor or small" mysteries of our lives and the world around us. This set of 56 cards is further categorized into four suits, namely:

- The Suit of Wands
- The Suit of Swords
- The Suit of Cups
- The Suit of Pentacles

Each of the four suits consists of 14 cards from numbers 1 (also called the Ace card) to 10 (10 cards) and four "court cards," including the Page, Knight, Queen, and King. While most decks have 78 cards, some have less or more. This book deals primarily with the 78-card deck. Later in this book, the Major and Minor Arcana cards are described in detail.

Types of Tarot Card Decks

The number of different types of decks available today is mind-boggling. There is a deck for every kind of practitioner and their likes or dislikes. Ranging from fandom characters to sports characters, there is no limit to the variety available today. Regardless of the pictures on the deck, each Major and Minor Arcana card's meanings and interpretations do not change. This chapter looks at some of the most basic types of tarot card decks that have withstood the test of time.

Rider-Waite

The Order of the Golden Dawn was one of Europe's most popular occult groups during the late 19th and early 20th centuries. Important occultists who were part of this group included Aleister Crowley, Arthur Waite, Pamela Coleman Smith, etc. Pamela Smith and Arthur Waite created the Rider-Waite (also called Rider-Waite-Smith) deck in 1909. Smith's illustrations for the deck were greatly inspired by the Sola Busca artwork, the earliest known tarot card deck dating back to the 15th century.

The Rider-Waite deck.
https://www.pexels.com/photo/tarot-cards-13321546/

Also, Smith was the first to use images, human figures, and other symbols for the Minor Arcana cards, which were, until then, represented by a collection of swords, cups, pentacles, and coins. All these elements added by Pamela Smith made the Rider-Waite a trendy and sought-after deck when it was first released. It continues to rule in the tarot world even today.

The Rider-Waite-Smith deck is great for beginners. It uses situational images on the cards that anyone can easily relate to. The pictures on the cards of this deck are designed to spark and light up your intuition and trigger an emotional response in your brain, both of which help you connect the message received to the question asked.

Thoth

Lady Frieda Harris illustrated the Thoth or the Crowley Thoth tarot deck under the supervision of the famous occultist Aleister Crowley interlinked his own philosophy into the deck's images and symbolism. It has an Art Deco design, and the deck gets its name from Thoth, the Egyptian god of learning, writing, and reckoning.

The Thoth deck.
Image by Luciana Paula da Silva from Pixabay *https://pixabay.com/photos/arcana-tarot-spiritual-oracle-4140879/*

This deck is the second-most popular deck in use after the Rider-Waite deck. The best feature of the Thoth deck is that it is filled with stunning images and brilliant symbolism. The designs are unique and quite different from the traditional Rider-Waite deck. Crowley released his deck with a book called "The Book of Thoth." The book analyzes the tarot deck with Egyptian influences, the Tree of Life, Tetragrammaton, etc. Here are some of the differences between the Thoth and Rider-Waite decks:

The Rider-Waite deck's imagery, influenced by Christianity, Paganism, and the ideas and stories of the Medieval Era, is very intuitive, making it perfect for beginners. It is easy to learn quickly about the cards and their meanings. The images and symbolism of the Thoth deck are drawn from ancient esoteric occultism. Therefore, understanding and interpreting the cards' meanings takes some time and practice compared to the Rider-Waite. Usually, a more experienced practitioner would use the Thoth deck.

Some of the card names are different too. For example, the Strength card in the Rider-Waite deck is the Lust card in the Thoth deck. Also, the Suit of Pentacles in the Rider-Waite deck is the Suit of Disks in the Thoth deck. Similarly, there are some more differences between the two decks.

Marseille

The Tarot of Marseilles was very popular in France during the 17th and 18th centuries for playing. It is believed to have been created in Milan before its popularity and use spread to France, Northern Italy, and Switzerland. Like any standard tarot card deck, the Tarot of Marseilles or Tarot de Marseille also has 78 cards. With its amazing images and pictures, this deck first led tarot cards from being a mere playing deck to using it for occult purposes.

The tarot of Marseilles.

As a beginner, you should start with the Rider-Waite deck, learn and master the art of tarot card reading, and then perhaps you can move on to the other decks.

Modern-Day Uses of Tarot Cards

Today, tarot cards are used in multiple ways and are not restricted as a divination tool.

Tarot helps improve your mental health - Reading and using tarot cards are spiritual practices that help to strengthen mental and spiritual resolve. Reading tarot cards during stressful times is useful to improve your understanding of the current, difficult situation and also your responses and reactions to it.

Anxiety and depression are common mental ailments today, calling for the nurturing care of the affected person's soul. Tarot cards are very useful to this end. They improve your self-awareness which, in turn, helps you deal with the problems you are facing objectively. Tarot cards help you understand the undercurrents causing the problems in your life.

Tarot offers a holistic approach to any form of therapy - A genuine tarot card reader and practitioner will not hesitate to guide clients to counseling therapy and to qualified medical practitioners for help. However, Tarot offers a holistic approach to all kinds of therapy by helping clients open their hearts and minds to issues beyond conscious levels.

Tarot card readings help to spark therapeutic conversations - A tarot card specialist picks up cards. When a particular card is drawn, the client may see an interpretation that may or may not match what the tarot practitioner says. However, the consonance or dissonance in thoughts of the two helps clients to open up and spark therapeutic conversations.

To end this chapter on tarot basics, Mark Horn, the author of the bestselling book "Tarot and the Gates of Light: A Kabbalistic Path to Liberation," had this to say about the insights obtained from tarot cards, *"Tarot does not predict the future. However, the cards give you an amazingly clear picture of your present and the future so that you can make informed choices for optimal outcomes."*

Chapter 2: Developing Your Psychic Powers First

The most important aspect of tarot card reading is the power of the reader's intuition. Psychic powers play a crucial role in accurate readings and interpretations of tarot card spreads, images, and drawings. Therefore, even before you pick up a deck, you must connect with, develop, and sharpen your psychic and/or intuitive powers.

It's important to sharpen your intuitive skills before attempting to read the cards.
https://unsplash.com/photos/D3SzBCAeMhQ

The Psychic Spectrum

Before moving on and explaining the psychic spectrum, it's a good idea to put aside some misconceptions about psychic or intuitive powers. Often, when people hear the word "psychic," their minds conjure up images of crystal balls. Sometimes, they think of neon-lit stores that lead to dark rooms in which an old woman sits with a crystal ball in front of her, a few animatronic contraptions to manipulate supernatural séances and experiences, fog machines, smoke screens, etc. Some have been trained to believe that the concept of "being a psychic" is a scam and that there is no truth in "extrasensory gifts."

The first step to tuning in to your psychic powers is to disconnect from these "scam" lessons that have been driven into human minds for years. Yes, there are frauds, con artists, and charlatans in the world of psychics, too, as there are in other industries and fields of work. These charlatans use fear or some other emotional blackmail to prey on vulnerable individuals. The book is not talking about such people when it speaks of "psychic powers."

A true psychic is someone with extrasensory gifts, meaning they can hear, see, feel, touch, and sense things and experiences beyond the physical world. A "normal" person may never be able to understand this ability with their thought process limited by the five senses. Most people are trained to recognize certain things in the physical world. For example, everyone knows the sky is blue or gray depending on the weather conditions. Many people can easily recognize happiness, sadness, anger, etc.

Human sensory experiences are all concretized into the material, tangible, or at least elements that they can easily feel. However, the deeper you try to dive into your sensory experiences, the more you'll realize that there are things you can sense that are not easily accessible to common people. When you keep diving deep into your "extrasensory powers," the more you will be able to access and harness the power of your psychic talent.

So, what is the ability to be a psychic? It is the ability to process sensory experiences and information at a deep spiritual, emotional, and mental level. A psychic could use both tangible and intangible stimuli. Of course, this definition is too narrow to cover the entire psychic spectrum because each of us is gifted with varying degrees of this talent. Therefore, the psychic spectrum is quite large and covers a lot right from small, seemingly insignificant sensory perceptions, like being able to sense cranky or angry moods in people, to much higher and subtler aspects that may appear magical to people with "normal" perception.

It may help to use an illustration to understand the concept of the psychic spectrum. Suppose four friends, Susan, Alia, Michael, and Nathan, meet for dinner. Susan arrives first, unhesitatingly asks the lady at the reception for her reserved table, and is led there quickly. When she sits, Susan notices her plate does not have a spoon, and the one next to her is missing a fork. Her glass is filled with water. But the glass at the seat opposite her is empty. She sips from her glass and waits for her friends to arrive.

Next, Michael enters the hotel and notices the receptionist is busy on her phone. He hesitates, wondering if she is angry or sad about her situation. Michael is sensitive and doesn't want to break into her thoughts abruptly. So, he gently coughs to grab her attention. She looks up from her phone and smiles at Michael, who is relieved that she is okay. He is also led to the reserved table. He greets Susan, and they reminisce while Michael browses through the menu, wondering what he should eat.

Ali walks into the restaurant, and the sensory experiences she feels assault her. She observes the loud and garish decor of the place. Ali notices how efficiently and quickly the servers are doing their job. She hears a guest complaining loudly on the phone somewhere at the back. After putting the phone down, he snaps at the lady next to him and the two kids sitting on the opposite sofa. She wonders how long the lady and the children will accept his arrogant behavior. Will the children grow into aggressive or docile adults? Suddenly, she hears her name being called and notices Susan and Michael waving to her from a table. She hurries to join them.

Nathan walks in last, and his feelings and experiences are far more than any of his three friends. He is utterly overwhelmed by the sights, sounds, smells, movements, and, thanks to the jacked-up air conditioner, the coldness in the air. He can even sense the interpersonal dynamics of two couples sitting at two different tables. Out of the blue, he feels sadness hanging in the air as if the place had accumulated pain and agony. Nathan wondered if some kind of bad accident had happened. Maybe deaths? Or a fire that killed people? He meets his friends, and they have a good time together. But Nathan can't shake off the feeling of dread right through the meal.

From the above example, you can see that four different people saw and experienced different things in the same setting and amidst the same stimuli. Each person's sensory abilities and range are different and unique. Use this example to understand your own sensory abilities. How much stimuli and energy do you absorb? What kinds of stimuli affect you the most, spiritually, mentally, and/or emotionally? When you connect with your own gifts and talents, you can delve deep and harness your psychic power.

How to Develop Psychic Powers

More than not, psychic powers get maximum exposure during childhood. These talents are usually passed on by those who are close, such as family members or even dear friends. For example, a child's mother may be tuned in deeply to her psychic powers, and she could teach her child how to use them.

Children tend to observe and notice far more than adults because, at that stage, survival instincts are strong. As they grow older, they are trained to "not be so sensitive." They are taught not to believe in "absurd" things like ghosts and spiritual beings. They are conditioned into disconnecting themselves from their intuitive powers. They are taught that emotions and extrasensory elements are anathemas to scientific logic and reasoning.

It is time to turn the tables, accept your innate gifts, and know that psychic powers are not "strange and opposite" to science and logic but are merely outside the current purview of scientific metrics. Instead of suppressing your inherent gifts, you should embrace them and learn to develop them.

Treat your psychic powers as a long-lost friend. How do you see old buddies from school you've met after a long time? They are all new people now, right? They may seem like strangers at the beginning of the second innings. And yet, when you sit and talk with them, old memories lost in your subconscious mind will emerge, and those seemingly broken bonds will be formed again, stronger and better than before.

Do the same with your intuitive powers. Reconnect with it as you would a beloved childhood friend. Your intuition has always been part of your spirit. It is just that it lies forgotten in the debris of life complications. Dig it up and connect with it again. Use these daily exercises for help.

Colors with Emotions

Connect your emotions with colors. Here's an example. Suppose you have had a difficult conversation with your boss. You are angry that they don't seem to see your point of view. Associate anger with a color of choice, say brown. Every time you are angry, visualize the color brown filling your mind. When you do this repeatedly, your intuition will register the association of the color brown with anger, which, in turn, will help you see emotions that are not obvious.

For example, if you are having an apparently normal conversation with your spouse. But you see the color brown. Then it could mean that there is anger in the environment. And since you are not angry, it means your spouse is angry about something. You can speak to your spouse about it.

As another example, suppose someone was trying to flirt with you, and you liked the feeling. You can associate the feeling of romance and love with pink. Keep connecting this emotion with this color as much as you can. Soon, your intuition will associate pink with love and romance. After a while, if you see pink when your friend or a family member is talking about another person, your intuition is telling you there is a romantic link.

Room or Space Scanning

Scanning the environment or space around you is an excellent way to build your psychic abilities. This exercise might appear to be a wee bit awkward initially. However, no one else will see your practice because it is entirely in your mind. Use these steps to help you:

- Stand anywhere in the room or space you want to scan, ensuring you can see clearly on all sides.
- You can either move around physically for the scan or use your eyes.
- Note the sights, sounds, smells, objects, etc., in the space.
- Notice the corners, the windowsills, the doors and windows, tables and chairs, and all other furniture.
- What are the things that are most inviting to you?
- What are the things you don't like in the room?
- What objects are giving you a negative vibe?
- Which ones are giving you a positive vibe?

Make mental notes of your feelings about all these things. Remember to write them down before you forget them. Repeat the scanning exercise everywhere, including outside spaces such as parks, malls, offices, subways, etc. The scanning exercise will help you increase awareness of your surroundings. The more you develop this awareness, the better your chances of noticing energy shifts.

When you have mastered space or room scanning, extrapolate the exercise to past memories and experiences. Remember to recall as many details as possible about good and bad experiences. What created the shift in the energy that led to the pleasant or unpleasant experience?

The mastery of scanning your past memories will eventually help you foresee future events and happenings. Experts opine that this is one of the most basic but powerful exercises that leads to astral projection or the ability to have willful out-of-body experiences. Astral projection takes years of diligent and patient practice before anyone can concretize it. Only those with extremely powerful psychic abilities can do it. However, the scanning exercise mentioned above is the first step toward it.

Dream Journal

Dreams are a portal between the physical world and the spiritual world and otherworldly realms. They connect your subconscious and conscious minds. Dreams help you reach out to innumerable memories that are deeply embedded in your psyche. People constantly create boundaries between their conscious and subconscious minds in the physical world. These boundaries are needed because of their limited sensory abilities.

Here's how boundaries help you in the practical world. Every moment, your senses are assaulted by a range of stimuli, and you can't ingest all of them. You would go crazy if you had to do so. Most of your sensory experiences and memories go straight into your subconscious mind, where they are stored for later use if needed.

Dreams are the best ways to connect with your subconscious mind and retrieve those memories. A powerful connection with your subconscious mind helps develop your psychic abilities. And so, dreams are excellent pathways for improved intuitive powers.

Dreams happen in a world that is completely free of all constraints. You can move around effortlessly in your dreams without any physical barriers, anywhere and everywhere. You can travel to foreign lands. You can do time travel and go into the past and future.

Dreams are a representation of an alternative reality. The more you dream, the more powerful your intuition will become and the more comfortable you will be dealing with your subconscious mind. With this, you'll realize and harness the power of the fluidity that exists between worlds. Use these tips to start and maintain a dream journal:

- Always keep a pen and paper near your bed so that you can write down what you saw in your dreams as soon as you wake up. Immediacy and speed are key aspects of maintaining accurate dream journals. If you wake up in the middle of the night after a dream, try to jot down the points you can recall before going back to sleep.

- Use the present tense to write your dream journal. Write it as if you are in a dream. When you do this, the chances of recalling as many details as possible from your dream are high.

- Do not forget to add the emotions you felt. Not only is the plot or events that took place in the dream important, but also how you felt. Did you enjoy what happened? Or did it scare you or fill you with sadness? Did you feel shame or embarrassment? Was the setting familiar?

Dream journaling helps you create a strong connection with your subconscious mind and facilitates lucid dreaming, wherein you can navigate through and control your dream. Manifestation of desires can be used through lucid dreaming.

Reading the Energy of Objects and People

Everything in this cosmos is made up of energy. All tangible and intangible elements in the universe, including objects, people, feelings, thoughts, and all else, are energy manifestations in different forms. So, if you can read and interpret the energy of any element, you can uncover the hidden secrets that the element holds in its core which is a direct advantage to building your psychic powers.

First of all, find out if you are an energy sponge or a source of energy. Only when you know this can you take control of the energy in your vicinity. Most people are unaware of how their energy impacts others and the space around them. Some people's negative energies can blanket an entire room, and unexpectedly and inexplicably, the room's mood can transform from happy to sad.

In contrast, people with happy, positive vibes can spread joy and love to everyone in their vicinity. It is obviously ideal to avoid or counter negative vibes and positive vibes. Reading the energy of people and things will help you with this.

Use these tips to develop your energy reading skills:

Focus on body language - When trying to read people's energy, focus on nonverbal aspects as much as the words they say. Pay attention to their eyes, the tone of their voices, how they shake hands with you, and the vibes they give out.

Focus on your feelings and memories for objects - What kind of memories does an object evoke? Does it make you feel sad, happy, or angry? For example, if you had a ring with a heart made of stones to symbolize your ex-partner, and that relationship ended badly, leaving you heartbroken, any heart-shaped objects similar to that ring could evoke sadness or, perhaps, resentment in your mind. The energy from that object aligns with your feelings and thoughts.

Chapter 3: Kabbalah and Tarot: A Mystical Connection

Kabbalah mysticism can help the reader peer through the mysticism hidden in tarot cards. Life and the entire cosmos consist of complex layers of interconnected matter and energy. Kabbalah is the science that helps us understand and unravel this vast interconnectedness. Kabbalah is an eternal, timeless science that goes beyond the limited notions of time, space, and physical limitations that human beings are accustomed to.

Kabbalah is a Hebrew word that refers to the study of the universe's fundamental laws that support existence and non-existence. Importantly, although Kabbalah is a Hebrew word, the study of it is not limited to just one religious group. The concept of interconnectedness, the core belief of Kabbalah, is available in varying forms across various cultures and religions of the world.

For example, in Tibetan Buddhism, philosophical ideas similar to what is explained in Kabbalah are collectively called Kalachakra. Even modern physics, especially the discoveries of quantum physics, match the ideas mentioned in ancient Kabbalah texts. Yet, modern physics has a long way to go before it can "prove" what the wise ancients already knew and recorded.

The Tree of Life

According to Kabbalah, the Tree of Life consists of ten Sephirot (singular - Sephirah). The Tree of Life consists of the Three Triads, namely

Intellect, Emotion, and Instinct Triads, laid out horizontally. These triads represent the flow of energy from the topmost, the Keter or Crown, which lies above the Intellect Triad, to the lowest Sephirah (the tenth one), the Malchut, beneath the Instinct Triad.

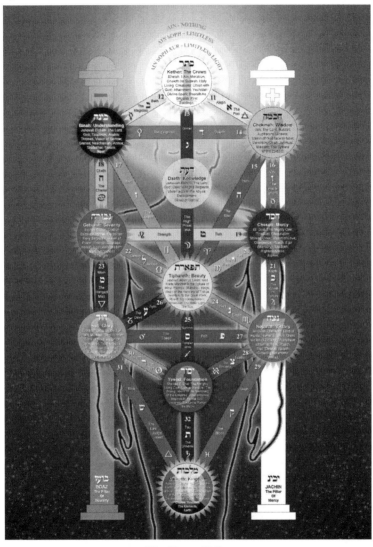

The Tree of Life.
Alan James Garner, CC BY-SA 3.0 <https://creativecommons.org/licenses/by-sa/3.0>, via Wikimedia Commons https://commons.wikimedia.org/wiki/File:Tree_of_Life_2009_large.png

Keter or the Crown is also called the "superconscious," an infinite field of energy and possibility. Keter is the ultimate state of being. It is the point touching the higher spiritual planes.

The energy flows through the Tree of Life and through each of the nine Sephirah until it reaches Malchut, representing the intention from the field of infinite possibilities to the space of finite manifestation.

The Intellect Triad

The Intellect Triad is the topmost rung in the Tree of Life and consists of the following three Sephiroth:

Chochmah - The Sephirah corresponds to the first seed of an idea drawn from Keter, the realm of infinite possibilities. The soul – the most ethereal aspect of the physical world, which conceives physical reality. Chochmah is referred to by many names, including inspiration, insight, inchoate awareness, etc., all of which point to that initial, almost imperceptible seed of thought that finds its way from the super consciousness into the topmost level of the consciousness.

Chochmah is the first flash of intellect or inspiration. It contains not only the seed of the idea but all the details as well. However, it is so concentrated that it appears only in its seed form while all else is obscured. The Chochmah is depicted as a dot containing all potential without actualization.

Binah - Binah is interpreted as understanding and refers to the state of the "seed idea" being fleshed out. It is the stage wherein the idea derived from the inspiration and insight of Chochmah gets a structure, and the story gets formulated. The color associated with Binah is dark red because it represents the color of congealed blood. In this context, blood is likened to the seed of an idea.

Binah also means to derive something from something else, to extract one thing about another. Binah expands and gives depth and breadth to the original seed of Chochmah. It is to be noted that Binah still only deals with the abstract potential contained in the idea.

Da'at - This Sephirah represents identifying with and connecting with the idea, structure, and associated story. The color of Da'at is gray because gray stands for intimate connection. Da'at is the Sephirah that enables abstract potential into actuality. The faculty of Da'at unites emotions and intellect. When you connect yourself with the idea so deeply that you become one with it, only then can you *feel for the idea* and get the power to bring it into actuality. This is the faculty of Da'at.

Emotion Triad

The fourth Sephirah is Chesed and is the first of the Emotion Triad. Chesed translates to unbounded love and mercy, which attracts and facilitates expansion, growth, widening the circle, and empathic concern. The color of Chesed is blue to symbolize the "flow," like the flow of blue water. Chesed is also referred to as loving-kindness, one that diffuses limitless compassion and benevolence.

Gevurah is the fifth Sephirah and the second in the Emotion Triad. It stands for strength and involves setting boundaries and limits, learning to say no, and finding focus. The color of Gevurah is red, the color that says "STOP" or "NO," which, in turn, means drawing limits or having limitations.

Gevurah is the attribute of control and restraint, concealing the infinite activating force of life and creation so that tangible entities can exist for human experience. Gevurah is also associated with law and justice so that Chesed or limitless kindness is distributed in a limited manner and according to one's merits. Gevurah's limits allow for creation and tangible reality to exist. Else, all and everything would have been nullified into the infinite Chesed.

Tiferet, the sixth Sephirah, stands for beauty and compassion. It stands for balancing and harmonizing opposing energies of all kinds. Tiferet's color is yellow, symbolizing the radiation of light. Tiferet harmoniously combines the faculties of Chesed and Gevurah, giving rise to beauty in the world. You can liken Tiferet to the heart in the center of your body, mediating between the right and left to create harmony and beauty.

Instinct Triad

Netzach is the seventh Sephirah and stands for victory. The word *Netzach* comes from "menatzeach," which means to "overcome" or "conquer." It represents the success of achieving your orchestrated intention after overcoming challenges and obstacles. The color of Netzach is purple, the color of dominance and power.

Hod is the next Sephirah in the Tree of Life. It represents surrender or submission, the exact opposite of the attributes of Netzach (overcoming and conquering). It tells you that letting go, giving in, and accepting are all ways of acknowledging what is beyond your control so that you can achieve your dreams. Orange, the color of hope and restoration, is the color of Hod.

Yesod is the last Sephirah of the Instinct Triad and represents twisting around and changing your truth until you find your authenticity. Yesod is the funnel through which the energy of the previous Sephiroth is channeled into the physical reality. The color of Yesod is green, which stands for renewal.

The last Sephirah is Malchut, the lowest one. It represents the culmination of the energy flow from Keter (the intangible superconsciousness) to the physical actuality. Malchut represents manifestation and expression. Its color is brown, the color of the earth and ground.

The Tree of Life is a map demonstrating the flow of intangible energy from infinite reality into tangible form. The Tree of Life urges us to find our deeper purpose and not merely get carried away by materialism. It tells you to dive deep and find the roots of your intangibles, which you can then harness into the physical world.

The Connection between Tarot and the Tree of Life

The Tree of Life represents the universal laws of reality. It stands for the eternal flow of the divine principle from the intangible realm into the physical reality governed by your five senses. The Tree of Life is not just somewhere out there; it lives in each individual. Your life is the microcosmic representation of the macrocosm. The echoes of the outside world are also found within you.

The flow of energy is upward as much as it is downward. If you follow the energy flow downward, you reach the physical manifestation of the intangible divine principle. If you follow it upward, you can find the divine source of infinite possibilities.

The 22 Paths of the Tree of Life and the Major Arcana

The Tree of Life consists of 10 Sephirot interconnected through 22 pathways, also called the Path of the Serpent. Each path connecting two nodes (or Sephirot) symbolizes the lessons you learn as you walk that path from one node to the connecting node.

The Path of the Serpent symbolizes a seeker's journey to reconnect with their lost divinity. The path represents the healing as one moves upward, longing to merge with the ultimate divine. The 22 pathways represent the growth and development as we walk through our internal world, similar to how the Major Arcana with 22 cards represents the Fool's Journey.

The Major Arcana symbolizes the evolution of the human spirit from ignorance to total enlightenment. It also represents the soul's return to its divine source, from matter back into spirit. The 22 cards of the Major Arcana are also related to the 22 Hebrew alphabets, namely Aleph, Beth, Gimel, Daleth, He, Vau, Zayin, Chet, Tet, Yod, Kaph, Lamed, Mem, Nun, Samech, Ayin, Phe, Tzaddi, Qoph, Resh, Shin, and Tav.

Here is a summary of the connections of the Major Arcana cards to their Hebrew and Kabbalah. As you learn more from the succeeding chapter, your understanding will get deeper and better.

The Fool's Card - Aleph - Primal Energy, unlettered, naive, and unaware. The Fool's Card represents the path between Keter and Chochmah.

The Magician Card - Beth - focus and attention to begin the journey toward learning and growth. It represents the path between Keter and Binah.

The High Priestess Card - Gimel - unconscious, uplifting. It stands for the path from Keter to Tiferet.

Empress Card - Daleth - nourishment, journey. It stands for the pathway from Chochmah to Binah.

Emperor Card - He - reasoning and vision - the path between Chochmah to Tiferet.

The Hierophant Card - Vau - Security, connections-path from Chochmah to Chesed.

The Lovers Card - Zayin - Cutting off, discernment, and the keen ability to distinguish accurately - the path from Binah to Tiferet.

The Chariot Card - Chet - Enclosure and separation - the path from Binah to Gevurah.

The Strength Card - Tet - twisting, surround - the path from Gevurah to Tiferet.

The Hermit Card - Yod - Work, action, and deeds - the path between Chesed and Tiferet.

The Wheel of Fortune Card - Kaph - grasp, hold, cover - the path between Chesed and Netzach.

The Justice Card - Lamed - Tongue, prod, dig - the path from Gevurah to Chesed.

The Hanged Man - Mem - Reversal, change over, overpower - Gevurah to Hod path.

The Death Card - Nun - Activity, life, revival, sprouting - Tiferet to Netzach path.

The Temperance Card - Samech - Principle, doctrine, support system - Tiferet to Yesod pathway.

The Devil Card - Ayin - Knowledge, lessons and skills, experience - Tiferet to Hod pathway.

The Tower Card - Phe - Words, speech, communication - Hod to Netzach pathway.

The Star Card - Tzaddi - Harvesting, fruition, integrity- Netzach to Yesod pathway.

The Moon Card - Quoph - Unseen, not obvious, hidden - Netzach to Malchut pathway.

The Sun Card - Resh - Redeeming, ultimate, finest - from Hod to Yesod.

The Judgment Card - Shin - Destruction, consume - from Hod to Malchut.

The World Card - Tav - The ultimate truth, covenant - from Yesod to Malchut.

Chapter 4: The Astrology behind Tarot

This chapter is dedicated to the astrological perspective of tarot cards. It will begin with enhancing your understanding of astrology.

What Is Astrology?

Astrology can be called "the language of the sky." It studies the movements of planets and stars and how they affect human life. It is the study of the connection between human events and celestial activity.

Astrology looks into the movement and patterns of stars and how they affect human life.
ESA/Hubble, CC BY 4.0 <https://creativecommons.org/licenses/by/4.0>, via Wikimedia Commons https://commons.wikimedia.org/wiki/File:A_home_for_old_stars.jpg

Celestial activities include the movement of the planets, stars, and zodiac signs. Human events include careers, relationships, achievements of dreams, and everything else humans desire. An astrologer practices astrology. There are multiple benefits of consulting an astrologer.

An astrologer can predict your future. This does not mean that you'll know the exact future outcomes. Based on the celestial activity, your astrologer can give you significant insights into your future. Nor can you really change your future. However, if the future is expected to be not-so-pleasant, then you can prepare yourself to make the best of it. If great things are expected, you can prepare to optimize the results as much as possible.

You can check your relationship compatibility. Strong relationships are formed between individuals whose thought processes and life expectations align more or less with each other. When your and your partner's physical, mental, and spiritual compatibilities are aligned, the chances of your relationship sustaining and growing from strength to strength are high. Astrology helps you with partner compatibility checks.

You can counter challenges and obstacles with the help of astrology. Astrologers can help you break down seemingly insurmountable obstacles and challenges into smaller, manageable portions by helping you deal with them one small problem at a time, based on celestial activity. You can learn about challenges waiting around the corner and prepare yourself to deal with them.

Planets and Their Significance

Different planets and other celestial bodies are connected to various aspects of human personality. The position of planets on your birth chart and their movements around your zodiac impacts your personality, how you think, and how you act and respond. Interpreting the significance of planets and their movements helps predict your future and understand your past and present.

Now, look at the connections between the seven planets according to western astrology: the sun, moon, Mercury, Venus, Mars, Saturn, and Jupiter.

The Sun - The Sun symbolizes the self and is the light of life on the earth. The Sun is associated with masculinity, creativity, self-expression, ego, vitality, and individuality. This planet represents a father figure, power, confidence, and authority. The position of the Sun on your birth chart determines how you deal with people. In a strong position, the Sun endows you with willpower and life-giving energy. It also represents your connection with your spiritual nature and your higher self. The Sun takes one month to move from one zodiac to another.

The Moon is the planet of emotions and is associated with personality traits like habits, behaviors, instincts, intuition, and femininity. It takes 2-3 days to move from one zodiac to the next. The Moon symbolizes your soul and your inner self. In a difficult position, the Moon can influence your moods and stability of mind negatively. The Moon makes you strong, courageous, and calm when placed in the ascendant house.

Mercury - Mercury deals with communication, ideas, and intelligence. It takes 3-4 weeks to move between zodiacs. Mercury rules over analytical skills, responsive and reactionary abilities, grasping and memory powers, and verbal and nonverbal communication. When Mercury is in the right place in your birth chart, your mental strength is great, and your ability to communicate is also very good.

Venus - Venus is the planet of beauty and rules over human activities such as love, relationships, pleasure, and art. Transiting from one zodiac to the next takes about 4-5 weeks. This planet of beauty symbolizes your love language and aesthetics. In your horoscope, Venus governs your personal taste, courtships, and relationships (both with people and finances).

Mars is the planet of action and takes about 6-7 weeks to transit between zodiac signs. It governs passion, aggression, libido, courage, desire, and competition. Mars rules over your determination and drive to get things done. The position of Mars in your life gives you insights into your energy, sexuality, and the dreams and desires that light you up. It also rules over your anger and, in a difficult position, can make your anger your biggest enemy.

Jupiter is the planet of expansion and is associated with wisdom, optimism, growth, property, and influence. It takes about 12-13 months to transit between zodiac signs; Jupiter showers you with luck, prosperity, health, and all the good things in life, provided it is in the right place in your horoscope.

Saturn is the planet of structure and governs karma, discipline, perseverance, obstacles, restriction, law, and justice. It is the slowest moving planet in astrology and takes about 2-3 years to transit between zodiac signs. Saturn is all about moral authority and obligations. When

Saturn impacts your life negatively (seemingly), it is a reminder that you need to handle your responsibilities and duties better, create boundaries for your safety, and know your karma is coming around.

Understanding the Zodiac

In addition to the planets, astrology is governed by the 12 zodiac signs (according to date of birth), which include:

- Aries (March 21 - April 19)
- Taurus (April 20 - May 20)
- Gemini (May 20 - June 20)
- Cancer (June 21 - July 22)
- Leo (July 23 - August 22)
- Virgo (August 23 - September 22)
- Libra (September 23 - October 22)
- Scorpio (October 23 - November 21)
- Sagittarius (November 22 - December 21)
- Capricorn (December 22 - January 19)
- Aquarius (January 20 - February 18)
- Pisces (February 19 - March 20).

Each zodiac sign mentioned above has a place in this cosmos; none is good or bad. They work together to render karmic outcomes. The 12 zodiac signs are categorized into four groups according to the four elements resulting in four types, namely fire signs, water signs, air signs, and earth signs.

Water signs, including Cancer, Scorpio, and Pisces, tend to be overly sensitive and emotional. They have powerful intuition, can be mysterious too, and rarely do anything garrulous. They thrive on intimacy and quiet, deep conversations.

Fire signs (Aries, Leo, and Sagittarius) are usually very temperamental and passionate, quick to anger, but equally easy to forgive and move on. They have abundant energy and are always on the lookout for adventure and ever-ready for action! Like the element they represent, they are very strong and inspire others to be their best.

Earth signs (Taurus, Virgo, and Capricorn) are not only grounded themselves but also keep the others downright practical and grounded.

They tend to have realistic perspectives but can be quite emotional too. They are deeply connected to materialistic things, perhaps due to their deep sense of practicality and logic.

Air signs (Gemini, Libra, and Aquarius) tend to be highly talkative and enjoy social interactions. They are also very rational and deep thinkers who analyze everything through their sharp intellects. They are book lovers who enjoy philosophical discussions. And yet, people born under the earth signs can also be quite superficial.

Now take a look at the characteristics of people born under each of the 12 signs.

Aries - The symbol of Aries is the head of a ram. Like the ram, people born under this sign are fiery (apropos to the fire element) and love competition. They dive first into all kinds of competition, often impetuously. Patience is not one of their virtues, but outright (even painful sometimes) honesty is. Like Mars, which rules over Aries, the people born under this zodiac are highly driven and always want to come first in everything they do.

Taurus - The bull's head represents this earth sign. Taureans love to relax in calm, peaceful surroundings. Like the bull, they love to soak for hours in water. They are persistent and loyal though they are often stereotyped for laziness and bullheadedness. Taurus is ruled by Venus, the planet of love, which makes Taureans one of the most sensual people.

Gemini - The symbol of this air sign is the celestial twins (sometimes, the Roman numeral II), and rightly so. They are so ambitious and want so many things that they are happy to lead two lives to achieve their dreams. Like the double life they like to lead, people born under Gemini are known to be as sociable and intelligent as indecisive and superficial. Mercury rules over this zodiac sign, so Geminis can absorb and process information faster than most people.

Cancer - Crab is the Cancer zodiac symbol. People born under this water sign are great at managing their emotional and materialistic realms with equal elan. Cancerians are charitable and friendly people. And yet, they can get crabbily and hurtfully blunt if you try to bring them out of their shells (or comfort zones). They are highly intuitive people and emotional sponges and will go to any lengths to protect themselves emotionally. Cancer is ruled by the Moon, which explains their highly emotional personality.

Leo - The lion is the symbol of Leo. Like the king of the jungle, Leos are loyal and passionate. Still, they can also be highly dramatic about everything involving them and enjoy basking in their own glory. Like the Sun that rules this sign, people born under this fire sign do not shy away from embracing their royal status. They manifest it through vivacity and their fiery attitude. While they are proud and brave, they tend to be highly aggressive and arrogant.

Virgo - This earth sign is symbolized by the Maiden, who represents the goddess of wheat and agriculture. Virgo is ruled by Mercury, the one who handles communication. Virgos are diligent, practical, logical, organized, and deeply connected with the practical world. They know how to get things done and done well. Their biggest drawback and strength is perfectionism. So, they are diligent in improving their skills and also end up worrying more than needed.

Libra - The balance scale represents this air sign. Librans are highly fixated on achieving equilibrium in every situation. Obsessed with symmetry, Librans chase balance wherever they go, especially in matters of the heart (which is not necessarily easy). They are known to be clever extroverts but hate being put in situations where they have to make hard decisions. Venus is their ruling planet.

Scorpio - People born under this water sign use emotional energy as their fuel to seek wisdom both from physical and spiritual realms. Scorpios (symbol is scorpion) tend to be powerful psychics making them appear elusive and mysterious. Thanks to their complicated and dynamic personalities, Scorpios are one of the most misunderstood zodiac signs. Mars rules over Scorpio, from whom they get their passion and aggression. If they have a cause to fight for, they are relentless and unstoppable, and no fear can hinder them in their path of achieving what they want.

Sagittarius - The adventurous Sagittarians love to travel everywhere in every form (physical, emotional, and spiritual journeys) in search of knowledge and wisdom, symbolic of blazing arrows. People born under this fire sign are extroverts; their enthusiasm and zest for life are infectious. Ruled by Jupiter, Sagittarians' great humor and intense curiosity make them winners in all their endeavors. Their biggest weakness is the absence of tact and diplomacy when dealing with the outside world and with people who are different from themselves.

Capricorn - The symbol of this earth sign is a mythological creature with a fish's tail and a goat's body. Patience, dedication, and perseverance are the hallmarks of the people born under this sign. This sign symbolizes dedication, responsibility, and time. Capricorns value tradition and are quite serious in their outlook. They make great leaders and can make solid, realistic, and well-executable plans.

Aquarius - Aquarius is a water sign, and people born under this sign are revolutionaries and highly progressive. The symbol of Aquarius is a water bearer, the harbinger of the source of life, water. Aquarians are dedicated to making this world a better place. They strive for the welfare of society and the world. They are deep thinkers who, although quite shy and reserved, do not hesitate to fight for a righteous cause. Saturn is the ruler of Aquarius.

Pisces - Symbolized by two fishes swimming toward each other in opposing directions, it reflects the dichotomous and conflicting perspectives that Pisceans tend to have between reality and fantasy. Being the last sign in the zodiac, it is as if Pisces has absorbed all the lessons taught by the previous 11 signs, thereby making Pisceans the most intuitive, wise, and empathetic person in the world. Ruled by Jupiter, people born under this water sign are friendly, selfless, and always ready to give a helping hand to those in need.

The Connection between Astrology and Tarot

Astrology and tarot are so closely connected that a combined form of predictive reading called *tarotscope* is very popular. Tarotscope is the art of reading an individual's horoscope through tarot cards. It is interesting to see how astrology and tarot are associated with each.

- Each of the 12 zodiac signs is associated with a Major Arcana card.
- Each number card in the Minor Arcana card is also associated with a zodiac sign.
- The court cards and aces are connected through the four elements, which, in turn, are connected to the 12 zodiacs.
- The Suit of Wands is associated with the fire element and, therefore, the three fire signs: Aries, Leo, and Sagittarius.
- The Suit of Cups is associated with the water element and, therefore, is connected to the three water signs Cancer, Scorpio,

and Pisces.

- The Suit of Swords is associated with the Air element and, therefore, with the three air signs Gemini, Libra, and Aquarius.

- The Suit of Pentacles is associated with the earth element and, therefore, with the three earth signs Taurus, Virgo, and Capricorn.

The associations of the Major Arcana cards, the 12 zodiac signs, and the planets are as follows:

- The Sun is Leo's ruler and is associated with the Sun card
- The Moon is Cancer's ruler and is associated with the High Priestess card
- Mercury, the ruler of Gemini and Virgo, is connected to the Magician card
- Venus, the ruler of Libra and Taurus, is associated with the Empress card
- Mars, the ruler of Scorpio and Aries, is associated with the Tower card
- Jupiter, the ruler of Pisces and Sagittarius, is associated with the Wheel of Fortune card
- Saturn, the ruler of Aquarius and Capricorn, is associated with the World card
- Aries is associated with the Emperor card
- Taurus is associated with the Hierophant card
- Gemini is associated with the Lovers' card
- Cancer is associated with the Chariot card
- Leo is associated with the Strength card
- Virgo is associated with the Hermit card
- Libra is associated with the Justice card
- Scorpio is associated with the Death card
- Sagittarius is associated with the Temperance card
- Capricorn is associated with the Devil card
- Aquarius is associated with the Star card
- Pisces is associated with the Moon card

- Cards 2, 3, and 4 (of all four suits) are associated with the cardinal signs: Aries, Cancer, Libra, and Capricorn
- Cards 5, 6, and 7 (of all four suits) are linked with the fixed signs, namely Taurus, Leo, Scorpio, and Aquarius
- Cards 8, 9, and 10 (of all four suits) are associated with mutable signs, namely Gemini, Virgo, Sagittarius, and Pisces

Combine all of the above connections and interconnections, and your tarot card reading will become more accurate, thanks to lateral associations with the elements of other equally powerful and popular predictive and divination tools.

Chapter 5: The Cards and Numerology

Tarot card reading is not just about memorizing what each of the 78 cards signifies. It includes multiple layers of understanding with direct and indirect connections with the querent's life and questions. Like Kabbalah and astrology, numerology is another useful tool for accurate and personalized interpretations of tarot cards. This section of tarot card reading is called Tarot Numerology. It will start by explaining the concept of numerology.

Understanding Numerology

What is numerology? Pythagoras, the ancient Greek mathematician, believed that, like other things in this universe, numbers are also endowed with energetic vibrations. And this is the basis for developing numerology as a divination, healing, and predictive tool.

Numerology is the study of numbers and how their energetic vibrations impact our lives. Every human is born with an inherent set of numbers imbibed into their personality or psyche. These numbers hold secrets and truths about people and indicate their life paths, challenges, and successes. Single-digit numbers from 0-9 form the foundational building blocks of numerology.

The most significant number that is part of every human is their Life Path Number based on the date of birth. This remains unchanged throughout an individual's life, greatly influencing your personality and how you live your life. Life Path Numbers show the challenges and opportunities you can get in your life. They reveal secrets about your personality that remain hidden deep in your psyche. Connecting with your Life Path Number will help you connect with your authentic self, which, in turn, will help you lead an authentic life instead of one driven by external stimuli.

Life Path Numbers

Before explaining what each Life Path Number represents and signifies, here is an illustration of how you calculate your Life Path Number. Suppose your birthdate is October 1, 1970. Begin by reducing each of your birthdate components into single digits.

The month is October which is 10 - 1+0 = 1

The date is 01, which remains = 1

Year is 1970 - 1+9+7+0 = 17 which is again reduced to (1+7) = 8

Then, add all the final signal digit numbers (1+1+8) = 10

And again, reduce this to 10 (1+0) = 1

So, your Life Path Number is 1.

1 - Number 1 is related to Aries, the first zodiac sign. People whose Life Path Number is 1 tend to be excellent leaders and innovators. The power of Aries' motivation drives them to become pioneers. Considering their outstanding leadership skills, the Ones tend to be very lonely people as they are most often found at the top of the ladder, strong but isolated and alone.

Conversely, their inherent desire for excellence can make them bossy, stubborn, and arrogant. They forget that no one lives on an island. You need support from other people. Playing second fiddle in any given situation is a huge challenge for Ones.

2 - Twos make excellent mediators and facilitators. The number 2 is connected with harmony, unity, and balance. The Twos can bring peace in a dissonant environment filled with friction and disharmony. Twos have powerful intuitions and can detect subtle energy shifts in any given environment, giving them the advantage of nipping the problem in the bud before it magnifies uncontrollably.

On the flip side, because Twos are so tuned in to harmony and balance, they find it very difficult to deal with frictions and conflicts and, therefore, end up under-appreciated. People often mistake Twos' compassion for weakness. This can be countered if Twos cease to seek external validation.

3 - Three is the expansion, growth, and fertility within a protected structure and/or framework to allow for growth and development without losing out to unbridled, dangerous freedom. People with 3 as their Life Path Number generally tend to have a positive, youthful outlook on life. They are zesty and love interacting with people, thanks to their excellent creative expression.

4 - In numerology, the number 4 stands for strength and efficiency. Interestingly, 4 is a much-feared number (1 3 adds up to 4). However, in truth, the number 4 carries wisdom and rationality on its head. It is a number that tells you to use your head rather than your heart to move forward. It is known to render stability and grounding in any concerned situation or for the concerned person. It also symbolized advancements but through the tried and tested traditional methods and not by anything new.

5 - "Curiosity killed the cat" is quite the opposite of the key characteristic of the number 5 in numerology. This number is driven by curiosity. People with 5 as their Life Path Number tend to be so curious to experience a variety of experiences in life to feel fulfilled. They crave adventure and freedom; the only goal they know to set is to get out there and experiment and experience. They are highly adaptable people and can fit into any kind of environment. On the flip side, Fives can be quite unreliable and non-committal.

6 - Number 6 represents the heart. It stands for unconditional support and love. People born with 6 as their Life Path Number are usually great nurturers and healers. They are highly empathetic and, in a group, are usually seen as harbingers of light and hope. They are great at letting others open up their hearts to them. They can be great friends and lovers. Conversely, the Sixes tend to be overly sacrificing and idealistic. When, practically, these things cease to work after a while, they tend to get resentful and angry.

7 - The number 7 stands for depth and is a number that does not deal with anything frivolous. People born with this Life Path Number tend to know that scratching the surface is not enough. You need to dig deep everywhere because gold is always buried deep. Therefore, the Sevens are always asking questions, finding more answers, doing relentless research, and using all their senses to collect as much information as they can.

Conversely, Sevens can be quite reclusive and secretive as they spend most of their time analyzing, researching, and digging deeper.

8 - Number 8 symbolizes achievements measured and tracked by the goals reached. People with 8 as their Life Path Number have a strong drive for success. They are highly ambitious and will work hard to realize their dreams only to dream more. Their primary goal is to achieve, and the best part is even during down periods, they find the strength to keep striving towards their goals. On the flip side, Eights can have a materialistic outlook with a bossy attitude.

9 - Nine in numerology stands for completion, or the ending of one cycle and the start of a new one. This number ushers a period of change and transformation. People born with this Life Path Number tend to be highly tolerant and spiritually awakened. They handle the pain with grace and dignity. They are highly supportive people too. On the flip side, Nines tend to indulge in excessive self-sacrifice leading to resentment and needless suffering.

Master Numbers

Certain numbers should not be reduced further into single-digit numbers. These are called Master Numbers and include 11, 22, and 33. People born under the aegis of these Master Numbers are believed to turn out very influential and successful. There is something very powerful about these three numbers that tend to heighten the person's potential to actualize their intuitive, intellectual, and materialistic goals.

11 - Number 11 in numerology is directly connected to intuition and the higher planes of wisdom. People born with 11 as their Life Path Number tend to be associated with their single-digit counterparts, namely 2 (1+1). Therefore, Elevens are also associated with harmony and empathy though they feel it far more deeply than the Twos. Also, Elevens share a few attributes of Ones, such as innovativeness and the desire to make a difference. On the flip side, Elevens can be quite overwhelmed by their empathetic nature, leading them to stress and depression, even self-doubt.

22 - Master Number 22 conjoins spirituality and materialism. The Twenty-Twos are endowed with the ability to receive profound insights and use them for the greater good. The single-digit companion of 22 is 4, the number associated with practicality and dedication.

Dedication is one of the biggest discerning elements that separate the Twenty-Twos from others. Hard work is deeply ingrained in their genetic and mental makeup. This dedication serves their personal purpose of achieving their goals and dreams and helpful attitudes toward humankind. They are continuously looking for ways to improve the lives of others.

On the flip side, because they are so hardworking and dedicated, they don't like to use up their energy for seemingly frivolous things such as emotions and the like making them seem like the "all work, no play" kind of people, which can be a big put off.

33 - Having a Life Path Number of 33 is very rare as it requires an uncommon combination of date of birth to get this. But those who have it become great healers and spiritual leaders. They become Master Teachers. They are selfless, often never thinking of themselves and always putting others before themselves. Altruism is deeply embedded in their psyche. Therefore, one of the biggest lessons that Thirty-Threes can learn is to keep themselves healed and happy so that they can be available for the amazing amount of good they can give to this world.

FAQs on Tarot Numerology

Why is numerology important in tarot reading? There are multiple reasons, some of which are shown below:

- If a number tarot card appears repeatedly, then there could be a strong indication of the numerical significance of that number rather than just the tarot card's meaning. Often, numbers appearing repeated in tarot card spreads represent the time or duration of an event or a situation.

- Suppose there are sequential numbers in a tarot card draw. In that case, it could indicate the start and the end period of an event, issue, or experience.

- Numerology gives additional nuances to tarot card spreads for more insightful and accurate readings than alone.

Here are some FAQs to help you understand better.

Q. What is the meaning of drawing an Ace in a tarot reading?

A. In tarot, the number 1 (or Aces) symbolizes the start of a journey. It tells you that everything is happening to facilitate the beginning of a new venture or journey for you. If you draw an Ace, it could signify the germination of a new idea or opportunity. An Ace in reverse (upside-down to the tarot reader and right-side-up facing the receiver) could mean that a great idea is there but is being blocked.

Q. What is the meaning of drawing Two in tarot?

A. Drawing a Two could represent the conjunction of two opposing forces to bring balance and harmony. Like the Twos who are always thinking of harmonizing environments of conflicts, drawing a Two could signify cooperating partnerships.

Q. What is the meaning of drawing Two in reverse?

A. If you draw a Two in reverse, it could indicate imbalance and disharmony in the concerned situation or relationship.

Q. What is the meaning of drawing Three in tarot?

A. Three stands for expression and growth. Drawing a three could indicate the end of one venture or phase and the preparation to begin the next one. As this number also stands for growth, it means you have achieved growth and progress in the previous phase and that you are moving toward your ultimate goal.

Q. What is the meaning of drawing Three in reverse?

A. In reverse, the Three card could indicate a time of self-isolation for self-improvement. Also, three stands for groups too. Therefore, a reverse three could mean it is time for you to stand alone, away from groups.

Q. What does 4 symbolize in tarot?

A. Four stands for stability, grounding, manifestations, and foundations. Drawing a Four card could indicate that your desires and dreams are being materialized or manifested. Four is a good sign for the Law of Attraction. But it does not mean that it is a period of sitting back and relaxing, thinking that all work is done. Work has to continue.

Q. What is the meaning of 4 in reverse?

A. Drawing a Four card in reverse could indicate a situation or person that lacks stability and grounding.

Q. What is the meaning of drawing a Five card?

A. In tarot, Five symbolizes instability and change, both of which might be unpleasant but necessary for growth. When you draw a Five card, it could indicate an upcoming change in dynamics or situation.

Q. What is the meaning of drawing a reverse Five?

A. If you draw a Five card in reverse, it could indicate a reluctance or resistance to face an upcoming, important challenge or obstacle that has a high chance of leading you to growth and development.

Q. What is the meaning of drawing a Six card?

A. In tarot, drawing a Six means it is a time for resting and healing. It indicates a time for harmony and cooperation.

Q. What is the meaning of drawing a reverse Six?

A. A reverse Six could indicate a time of imbalance and disharmony.

Q. What is the meaning of drawing a Seven?

A. In tarot, drawing a Seven usually means a time to reflect and assess before proceeding further.

Q. What is the meaning of drawing a reverse Seven?

A. A reverse Seven could mean a lack of clarity or focus or an overwhelming amount of confusing options.

Q. What is the meaning of drawing an Eight card?

A. In tarot, Eight represents accomplishment and mastery. Like the infinity symbol, 8 represents eternal motion and flow. If you draw an Eight, it could indicate the need for continuous striving and work to achieve the desired goals.

Q. What is the meaning of drawing a reverse Eight?

A. Drawing an Eight in reverse could indicate the lack of hard work to achieve desired results and/or the absence of material success.

Q. What is the meaning of drawing a Nine card?

A. In tarot, drawing a Nine could indicate fulfillment and completion. It means the rewards of hard work can be expected.

Q. What is the meaning of drawing a reverse Nine?

A. Drawing a reverse Nine could indicate a lack of fulfillment and closure.

Chapter 6: Meet the Cards I: Major Arcana

It's now time to take a closer look at each of the cards in the tarot deck. The chapter starts with the 22 cards of the Major Arcana. Let's dive right in.

The Fool

The Major Arcana begins with the Fool, a metaphor for naivety and innocence. This card represents each person in their life journey as they start with innocent faith and take their first step eagerly despite knowing that the journey is rife with struggles and obstacles. The Fool's card represents the beginning, a fresh and spontaneous beginning. The Fool depicted on the card with his arms flailing wide and his head held high with hopes is a symbol of a simple soul ready to embrace everything that comes his way.

The fool.

The Fool stands at the edge of a cliff but is totally oblivious to the dangers ahead. He is completely unaware of all the dangers and hazards that the journey has in store for him. He is just totally happy to take what comes his way. The Fool is more or less outside the other cards of the Major Arcana and is like the number 0, which stands in the middle of positive and negative integers. Like zero, the Fool represents nothingness or emptiness and gets filled with desires and feelings as he undertakes his journey.

The Fool's card represents the entire cosmos and all the planets and zodiac signs because he stands for nothingness which holds everything. In the concept of a journey, the Fool stands for the conception of an idea or thought. The keywords of this air tarot card are innocence, free-spiritedness, risk-taking, and adventure.

The Fool is the first path between Keter and Chochmah. Keter or the Crown is Pure Spirit and is symbolized by a mere point but one that has infinite potential. However, it embodies everything in this cosmos. Keter needs to act for the process of creation to begin. So, Keter moves forward and thrusts itself on Chochmah (or Wisdom).

In the same way, the Fool represents infinite potential. This card is the first step that the soul has taken toward entering the cosmos from Nothing (or Zero) to something. The Fool's path represents the complex transformation of 0 to 1 or something, which is the beginning of the tangible universe.

Drawing an upright Fool usually indicates the start of a new journey. During this time, you are likely to feel euphoric and excited without any constraint. If you draw a reverse Fool card, it could indicate a time of danger wherein an action is taken without considering the consequences. It could also mean that you are living in the moment without any plans for the future, which may be a good or bad thing.

The Magician

The second of the 22 Major Arcana cards is depicted with a magician who represents the positive and masculine side of creativity. The Magician represents conscious awareness, a force that empowers people to create through the sheer use of willpower.

The magician.
https://pixabay.com/es/illustrations/el-mago-cartas-de-tarot-tarot-mago-6103696/

The Magician's right-hand points upward to the sky. His left hand is turned downward, facing the earth. This symbolism translates to "As above, so below," a phrase pregnant with multiple meanings, including the following:

- Earth is a reflection of heaven
- The external world is a reflection of our inner world
- The microcosm is a reflection of the macrocosm

The Magician also indicates that he can mediate between the tangible and intangible worlds. On his table are the four suits of the Minor Arcana, each representing the four elements, fire, air, water, and earth. Therefore, the Magician is a master of all four elements. The infinity symbol hovering above his head represents the infinite possibilities when one's will and spirit are strong.

This card represents the Number 1, which symbolizes unity. So, the Magician is adept at his craft and a student continuously seeking lessons from the world. The power of the Magician is knowledge, and he is a relentless seeker of this power. He indicates that magic happens when you can bend your will to realize your intangible dreams into tangible outcomes and goals.

The keywords associated with the Magician card are desire, willpower, concentration, focus, and the manifestation of desire through skills and knowledge. Drawing an upright Magician card could indicate that you are ready to achieve your fullest potential, and it is time to delve deep into your willpower and make things happen. If you get a Magician card, it means you must not hold back anywhere lest you let go of opportunities that come knocking on your doors.

In reverse, the Magician card could indicate wasted talent, manipulation, cunningness, deception, and trickery. Drawing a Magician card in reverse could indicate a time of care and caution because you could be lured by deception and illusion. All may not seem as is, and it could be that someone is trying to manipulate you into a trap.

The Magician is associated with Mercury, which rules over Gemini and Virgo. In the process of creativity, the Magician card represents incubation, wherein the idea is slowly but steadily finding ways to concretize in the tangible world. It is connected to the air element. In Kabbalah, the Magician card is the path between Keter and Binah and indicates the start of material production. The Magician is the director of channeled energy.

The High Priestess

The keywords for an upright High Priestess card include intuition, mystery, inner voice, spirituality, unconscious mind, and powers associated with the higher planes of consciousness. In reverse, the Empress card implies hidden motives, superficiality, repressed intuition, and confusion.

The high priestess.

The High Priestess is depicted as sitting on a cube-shaped stone placed between two pillars. In addition to symbolizing the female-male, good-evil duality in nature, these two pillars symbolize Jachin, the Pillar of Establishment, and Boaz, the Pillar of Strength associated with the Temple of Solomon.

That she sits between the two pillars signifies her mediatory skills through which she maintains the balance between two opposing forces.

Suppose you draw an Empress card in your tarot reading. In that case, it indicates listening to your intuition and not only relying on your intellect to get things done. In fact, drawing an Empress card should compel you to put your intuition above your intellect in the given situation. It indicates using mediation, prayers, and spiritual work for the concerned query.

When the High Priestess comes into your reading, it means she is calling you to listen to what she says, trust her, and follow her into the balanced world of opposing forces that might seem frightening initially. Still, it will lead you to great success and happiness. She is calling upon you to seek answers within yourself.

If you draw a reversed High Priestess card, it could indicate that you find it difficult to listen to your intuition. It tells you that you have been ignoring your instincts and need to reconnect with them in new ways because the "rational" approach will not work for the current situation. A reverse High Priestess indicates that you must not be afraid to ask yourself pertinent and difficult questions so that new paths to your intuitive powers can be lit to find your way in the dark.

Interestingly, the Fool meets both the Magician and High Priestess almost immediately at the start of his journey. These two cards balance each other, the Magician's positive, active, masculine elements with the High Priestess's negative, mysterious, feminine elements. It is important to know positive and negative do not have a "good" or "bad" meaning in tarot. They are merely opposite but of equal value and stature. Both positive and negative are imperative elements for balance and structure in this world.

The High Priestess is associated with the Moon and is, therefore, connected with the water signs, namely Pisces, Cancer, and Virgo. In Kabbalah, she is the path that connects Keter to Tiferet, the path connecting the Pure Spirit to beauty and harmony. The name of this path is gimel which means "camel," the self-sustaining animal of the desert that can survive for days on end without water. In the same way, the High Priestess can draw energy from the depths of her being to harness a huge reservoir of self-confidence and intuitive powers to cross the path.

The Empress

The third Major Arcana card depicts a queen sitting on a throne surrounded by nature's abundance in the form of rivers and streams and an enchanting verdant forest. The Queen on this card also symbolizes

Mother Nature and/or the fertility goddess. Her robe, designed with pomegranate patterns, represents fertility (a pomegranate is full of seeds, so it stands for fertility). Aptly, the element governing the Empress card is earth.

The empress.
https://pixabay.com/es/illustrations/emperatriz-carta-de-tarot-s%c3%admbolo-6016923/

Venus rules the Empress, and therefore, it is the epitome of love and harmony. The figurine on the Empres's card has blonde hair with a crown of stars, a symbol of her connection to the magical, mystical realms. The Empress is a harbinger of blessings and abundance.

The keywords of an upright Empress card are nature, fertility, nurturing, motherhood, supportive, sensual, and/or committed romantic relationships. An upright Empress card indicates connecting with our femininity and sensuality to attract happiness and joy into our lives. The Empress is connected to Venus and, therefore, is associated with the Libra zodiac sign.

If you draw an upright Empress card, it means it is a time of self-care and self-compassion. It is also a card of pregnancy and motherhood. Of course, you must check out the cards in the entire spread to confirm this. Alternatively, it could indicate receiving or giving motherly, nurturing love. The Empress card also indicates new beginnings, including a new venture, idea, or project.

Reversed Empress card could indicate a loss of willpower, self-reliance, and inner strength because you have used up a lot of energy in caring for the welfare of others. A reverse card might mean that you need to stem the flow of excess nurturing and concern for others lest it goes overboard and you end up neglecting your own needs. Excessive concern for others could also result in smothering people you love with your care despite meaning well.

In Kabbalah, the Empress connects Binah and Chochmah, the path of the unity of the masculine and feminine. This is why the Empress is depicted as pregnant in some tarot decks. She unites the male and female to bring forth new life. Also, the Empress is the universal womb of creativity.

From the point of view of the Fool's journey, when he encounters the Empress, he recognizes the loving maternal figure, the one who nourishes and loves him unconditionally. He also learns about and feels grateful for Mother Nature, who showers her abundance on him. Like a baby who loves exploring new sensations and experiences, the Fool cannot stop exploring everything that enchants his senses.

The Emperor

The Emperor tarot card is depicted by a stoic ruler sitting on his throne, decorated with four rams' heads, the symbol of his zodiac sign, Aries. He carries a scepter in his left hand, symbolizing his right to rule. The orb that he carries in his right hand represents his kingdom. He is also depicted with a long, flowing beard representing his years of experience and the wisdom, knowledge, and authority he has gained to be the Emperor.

The emperor.

The mountains behind him stand for his ambition and determination to greater leadership capabilities. These depictions are exactly opposite to the Empress card, which shows flowing rivers, nurturing care, and life-giving kindness and love. On the other hand, the Emperor rules with grit, determination, and sheer masculine force.

The keywords for the upright Emperor are structure, stability, protection, control, authority, and discipline. In reverse, the Emperor symbolizes tyranny, domineering control, stubbornness, and lack of focus and discipline. Drawing an upright Emperor card could indicate that, like him, you should be a strategic thinker for the problem at hand. You should create rules and regulations and think in a structured manner for optimal benefits.

Like the element fire that rules the Emperor, he is a reminder that you should guide but with a firm, authoritative hand lest things go out of control. It is also a reminder that although you might be in a position of power, like all kings and emperors, you are also here to serve the people you rule over. It is a call to act rationally and put your intellect over your mysterious instinctive powers. The Emperor in any of your tarot card sightings calls for you to break free from the shackles and limiting beliefs that bind you down.

Drawing an upright Emperor card indicates success in the future as you achieve your goals determinedly, methodically, and strategically. Suppose any of your cards depict the Emperor. In that case, it could indicate you'll soon be given a position of power, where methodical structure and order are needed for successful outcomes. You are to bring your years of wisdom and experience to the table to take it forward.

If you draw a reversed Emperor card, it could indicate the abuse of authoritative power. It could manifest in your life as an authoritative father, possessive partner (on the personal front), or an overly controlling boss (in the workplace). It could also mean that you are not as strong as a ruler and that you must take corrective action to that end.

In Kabbalah, the Emperor is the path between Chochmah and Tiferet. In this context, Chochmah is Wisdom (or the father figure), and Tiferet is the son. The father takes the manifesting energy from the Empress and passes it on to the individual, his son. The Emperor (masculine energy) and Empress (feminine energy) together bring about beauty and harmony in the world.

The Hierophant

The Hierophant card depicts a religious figure (could be the Pope or a leader of any religion) sitting in a formal religious environment like a temple or church. The initiating religious priest is shown wearing elaborate religious vestments. His right hand is depicted as being raised in blessing and benediction. He carries a cross with three horizontal lines representing the Trinity in his left hand. Two disciples or acolytes are seen sitting at his foot, learning from him.

The hierophant.

https://pixabay.com/es/illustrations/el-hierofante-tarot-tarjeta-magia-6016942/

The Hierophant, or the High Priest (ruled by Taurus and associated with Jupiter and Venus), is the male counterpart of the High Priestess. An upright Hierophant card keywords are conventionality, tradition, conformity, beliefs, knowledge, wisdom, and social groups. The keywords for reverse High Priest include unconventional, ignorance, new and untried methods, rebellion, and non-conformity.

Drawing an upright Hierophant card could indicate a desire to conform and follow set rules and regulations. It is an indication to stick to conventional methods and within orthodox boundaries. It is good to adapt to existing beliefs instead of trying innovation and newness.

Seeing a Hierophant in your tarot sightings could mean you'll be involved in religious ceremonies and rituals. This card clearly indicates well-established institutions and belief systems and tells you that you should stick to conformity and not break tradition for optimal outcomes.

Drawing a reversed Hierophant could indicate a feeling of being restricted or constrained by systems and structures. You might be experiencing a feeling of being trapped and that you have lost control of your life. You desire flexibility and want to break free from the shackles of tradition and convention. You feel tempted to break orthodoxy and turn rebellious. You feel the urge to defy social norms.

If you draw a reversed High Priest card, it mostly means you want to question well-established traditions and doctrines. In a love relationship, drawing a reversed Hierophant might indicate a stalemate in your relationship. On the professional front, it could mean having a stifling work atmosphere.

In Kabbalah, the Hierophant card is the path that connects Chochmah and Chesed. The main function of the High Priest is to connect the "As above, so below." He represents the Great Teacher of mysteries and secrets and unlocks the understanding between illusion and our sensory experiences.

The Lovers

The Lovers card is depicted with a male and female pair of humans who are being blessed and protected by an angel from above. The happy, loving couple is in the midst of a beautiful garden. The fruit tree with a snake hiding it standing behind the couple clearly indicates that it is the Garden of Eden, where the snake is trying its best to tempt the happy couple to fall into the trap of the pleasures of the flesh.

The lovers.

Gemini is the zodiac sign, Mercury is the planet of the Lovers card, and the air is the element. Air is the element of communication and mental activity, both of which are crucial for relationships and partnerships. The angel's blessings that fall between the couple appear to give a sense of balance to the lovers.

The keywords for upright Lovers are union/love/relationships and partnerships/ romance/and choices. The most important interpretation of the Lovers card is that the confidence, trust, unity, and love given to each other by the couple empowers them both, strengthening their relationship. The bond between a loving couple is strong and intimate.

Another important interpretation of the Lovers card is that of choice. It tells us we all must choose between opposites and mutually exclusive things. So, if you draw a Lovers card and love may not be the answer you seek for your question, then the indication could be that you are in a dilemma and have to consider all things carefully before making your choice.

The Lovers card is a step forward from the Hierophant card, which is all about rendering structure and order and following set rules and regulations. For the Fool, he has two new experiences with the Lovers card. For one, he experiences the power of sexual union with another person and learns the desire to create relationships. Until now, the Fool was more or less self-centered. But when he encounters the Lovers card, he feels the urge to reach out and become half of a loving couple.

Second, he has also to include decision-making in his life lessons. It teaches him that he needs to weigh all options before him, find out what values he stands for, and then make appropriate choices. He yearns to learn and grow by making his own choices.

In Kabbalah, the Lovers card is the path connecting Tifereth to Binah, signifying the connection between the heart (or the solar center of the self) to the great confluence of super consciousness. The Lovers card represents the union of the sun (masculine) and moon (feminine) energy.

Drawing a Lovers card could indicate that you found out what is important to you and made the correct choices. The Lovers card helps you develop your sense of purpose. A reverse Lovers card keywords include imbalance, disharmony, wrong choices, indecisiveness, conflicts, and detachments.

A reversed Lovers card could mean an internal or external conflict you are dealing with. Disharmony and imbalances might be making your life difficult. It indicates it is time for you to take a step back and take corrective measures before moving forward.

A reverse Lovers card could also indicate a breakdown in communication in your professional and personal relationships and partnerships. It could indicate that you are not taking responsibility for your actions and choices. You could be blaming others for your decisions instead of accepting the onus for the consequences of those decisions that are fructifying at this point in time.

The Chariot

The Chariot card is depicted by a charioteer seated inside his vehicle driven by two sphinxes, one black and one white. The warrior wears a crown on his head, a depiction of enlightenment. A crescent moon on his shoulders guides him on his way. The ambiance is that of a blue sky adorned with twinkling stars. The water element governs the card.

The chariot.
https://pixabay.com/es/illustrations/carruaje-tarot-tarjeta-magia-6016921/

A square emblazoned on the charioteer's chest keeps him stable and grounded. The black and white colors of the two sphinxes symbolize two opposing forces the rider has to control to bring about balance and stability to achieve his life purpose.

Keywords for the Chariot are determination, success, drive and ambition, self-control, discipline, and willpower. The Chariot card talks to you about overcoming challenges and obstacles to achieve your goals. It tells you that you can become victorious if you learn to control what is happening around you and that strength and determination are key elements in this journey.

If you draw a Chariot card, it indicates maintaining focus and discipline to achieve your dreams. The card indicates that the path to your destination will be full of twists and turns, and an ordered, structured approach is critical for success. The Chariot could indicate that you'll likely display stamina and confidence in your life. A hitherto hidden, aggressive aspect of your personality could find its way out to feed your confidence. While aggression is useful sometimes, it should also be reined in so you don't lose control over it.

Keywords for reversed Chariot are lack of direction and control, powerlessness, and forceful aggression. If you draw a reversed Chariot, it could mean you lack confidence and aggression in the current situation. The reverse card tells you that you are so caught up in your goals that you are not thinking things through in a structured manner. You are allowing your impulses to take control of your actions.

A reversed Chariot card could mean you do not have control over your life, and opposing forces are controlling you. It means you are taking things lying down because of which life is taking you where it pleases. It is a reminder you need to take charge of your chariot and drive it to the destination you want in the way you want.

In the Fool's journey, he has become an adult with a strong sense of identity by the time he reaches the Chariot card. He also has some mastery over himself and has developed the tools and skills needed for success and materialistic happiness. The Chariot represents the Fool's ego, his largest achievement so far. The charioteer is a proud man sitting confidently on his vehicle, riding victoriously toward his goals. He is the master of all that he surveys and appears to be in visible control of everything around him. He is filled with self-satisfaction and self-confidence for the moment, at least.

The Moon and the Cancer zodiac sign govern the Chariot. In Kabbalah, the Chariot is the path that connects Binah and Gevurah, the path through which the Spirit descends to manifest in the tangible world of human beings. In the reverse direction, the Chariot, after conquering the lower planes, is all set to cross the lower part of the Tree of Life and move into the higher planes of spiritual consciousness.

Strength

The Strength card is depicted by a woman who is fearlessly and confidently holding open the jaws of a ferocious lion. The woman dominates over the menacing lion, yet she is calm and confident, showing signs of total control of a given situation. She is courageous and yet shows love and compassion. The lion itself is a symbol of strength and courage, both of which are critical for the success of human beings. However, if these two elements are not reined in or checked in, then they could lead to destruction and chaos.

Strength.
https://pixabay.com/es/illustrations/tarot-cartas-de-tarot-fuerza-6129685/

The keywords of this card are confidence, bravery, inner power, and compassion. Drawing an upright Strength card means you have the courage and fortitude needed to get through the difficult times ahead. It indicates you have the calm and peace needed to overcome obstacles and challenges, becoming stronger and braver. It also shows you are very compassionate and kind, willing to take people along with you.

Patience is your forte as you wade through challenges to achieve your goals and dreams. Your fearlessness and resilience are your great strengths in your life path. Drawing an upright Strength card means that even though you might be going through a difficult time right now, your bravery and confidence will see you through. Success and stability will be your companions sooner than later.

The keywords for the reverse Strength card are lack of or low confidence, cowardice, self-doubt, aggression, and inadequacy. If you draw a reverse Strength card, it could indicate a time of fear and strife. You might find it difficult to harness your inner strength and power – and that fear and uncertainty may be ruling your life. A reversed Strength card could also mean that you are dealing with depression and sadness for some reason, because of which happiness and positive energy are being drained from your life.

The zodiac sign associated with the Strength card is Leo, and the element is fire. In the journey of the Fool, the Strength card plays a crucial role. He dips into its power time and again to deal with the challenges and obstacles he finds on his way. He begins to think that he may not be the master he thought he was.

His ego may have grown, but there is a lot more to learn and master in this world. His aggression and confidence sometimes take a beating, which is when he learns the value of patience, compassion, and kindness from the Strength card. He learns that willful and determined commanding attitudes must be balanced with tolerance and kindness for true happiness. The Fool learns to tame his ego.

In Kabbalah, the Strength card is associated with the path between Chesed and Gevurah. This path calls upon people to tame their animalistic instincts and embrace mercy and compassion to connect with their higher selves. It is the path that teaches you to lose your ego and get rid of arrogance and pride to move forward in life.

The Hermit

The Hermit card depicts an old man standing alone on a mountain peak with a lantern in his right hand and a staff in his left hand. The mountain represents his achievements and accomplishments. The peak represents his knowledge and the wisdom he has garnered through his experience. The lantern has a 6-pointed star inside it, the Star of Solomon, which stands for wisdom. Therefore, the Hermit is a symbol of spiritual achievement rather than materialistic success. The staff he holds represents the Hermit's authority and power.

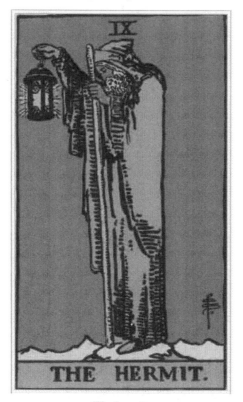

The hermit.
https://pixabay.com/es/illustrations/ermita%c3%b1o-tarot-tarjeta-magia-6016941/

The keywords for an upright Hermit card search for the authentic self, solitude, self-reflection, contemplation, and introspection. Seeing a Hermit card in your tarot sightings could indicate periods of solitude (not isolation or rejection). This time is for turning inward and seeking answers to your questions from within.

You must disconnect yourself from the crowds and the noise of your dreams and desires that threaten to throttle you. Step back from the noise and look within and seek answers. The Hermit card is a sign of walking alone through the darkness of your unconscious mind to find your true self.

If you draw a Hermit card, you desire solitude for contemplation and self-reflection. These moments of solitude help to clear the clutter of daily life so that you can reconnect with your true purpose and readjust your life path. It could also mean that a mentor or a coach could enter your life to help you.

A reversed Hermit card relates to loneliness, anti-social feelings, reclusiveness, isolation, and rejection. A reversed Hermit might mean you want to be left alone, which might be good. However, if not done correctly, being and feeling alone can lead to wrong outcomes for yourself and your loved ones.

Turning inward without proper support could lead to dangerous situations. People are known to have lost their sanity as they delved too deep into their psyche for their own good. The subconscious mind has dangers lurking to lure you into its abyss. Therefore, you must balance your inward search with support from fellow human beings.

From the point of view of your professional life, drawing a Hermit card could mean it is time to get to the bottom of something that has been bothering you for some time. Something needs to be done, and you have to get down to it before it takes on an uncontrollable element in your life.

In the Fool's journey, the Hermit card reminds us of the "Why" of human life. This card reminds him to find the true purpose of his life. Why is he here at all? He wants to know the answer not just to satiate his curiosity but with a deep desire to find his authentic self. With the Hermit card, the Fool turns inwards and digs deep into his emotions and thoughts, seeking answers. The sheen of the outside world is not attractive to him anymore, and he seeks something deeper and more meaningful. The Fool must undertake this journey alone.

The Hermit card is associated with Mercury, the zodiac sign Virgo, and the earth element. In Kabbalah, the Hermit card is the path from Tiferet to Chesed, the path of communication with the higher spiritual self. It is the path the lower self must undertake to find his authentic inner self.

The Wheel of Fortune

The Wheel of Fortune has a giant wheel in the center, which an eagle, angel, and bull surround, and a lion connected with four fixed signs, namely Aquarius, Scorpio, Leo, and Taurus. The four animals have wings which could indicate that they represent the four evangelists of Christianity.

Wheel of fortune.
https://pixabay.com/es/illustrations/tarot-cartas-de-tarot-6129686/

All four of the animals hold books in their hands which is symbolic of the Torah, the ultimate book of wisdom and knowledge. A lone sphinx rides on the giant wheel in the center. This is symbolic of cycles in your life. Sometimes, you are at the bottom, and sometimes at the top.

The Wheel of Fortune is associated with Saturn, the planet of structure and order, and the fire element. The upright Wheel of Fortune keywords are transformations, cycles, decisive periods, unexpected events or happenings, luck, and fortune. If you draw a Wheel of Fortune, it is a reminder that the cycles of life are not in your control. Everyone, from beggars to kings, is caught in these cycles, and none can avoid them. You must only learn to live in the moment and embrace everything happening in your life without resistance.

If you are in a good situation, then a bad one might come when the wheel turns, and the same thing is good when you are in a difficult situation. It reminds us that forces much larger than human forces are at work here, and we should give in to them. Regardless of where you land, the wheel will turn, and your position will change.

The keywords for a reversed Wheel of Fortune card are lack of control, bad luck, controlling or clinging to control, unpleasant delays, and changes. Drawing a reversed Wheel of Fortune indicates that good luck has not been in your life for a while now, and misfortunes have been following you. It reminds you that you are not in control and that you must simply wait for the wheel to turn again for better times.

It is important to remind yourself not to cling to control because bigger forces outside your purview of control are working here. Learn to let go and move on. The feeling of acceptance drives the wheel for another cycle with new positions for you and others.

From the point of view of the Fool's journey, he sees how things in this world are all interconnected. He has a vision of the world's design and how it moves on the Wheel of Fortune. He sees the intricate patterns and cycles that impact and affect us in different ways. He sees the universe in all its mysterious layers working together harmoniously. The Fool recognizes the importance of destiny and fate in his life and learns to embrace them wholeheartedly and without resistance.

In Kabbalah, the Wheel of Fortune card represents the path between Chesed (Mercy) and Netzach (Victory). The path connects the tangible personality to the higher, spiritual self through the pillar of mercy. The wheel symbolizes relentless cycles of birth, death, and rebirth.

The Justice Card

Astrologically speaking, the Justice card is associated with Libra, the zodiac sign of the balance and the air element. The Justice card speaks of law, truth, and fairness. The Lady of Justice sits on her judgment seat, holding scales in her left hand. The scales signify the importance of balancing logic with intuition to make accurate judgments.

Justice.
https://pixabay.com/es/illustrations/tarot-cartas-de-tarot-justicia-6129675/

The Lady of Justice stands for impartiality which is depicted by the double-edged sword she carries in her right hand. The square on her crown signifies clarity of thought, a key element during the dispensation of justice.

The upright Justice keywords are karma, accountability, consequences of actions, integrity, law, truth, and justice. If you draw the Justice card, it is a reminder that all your actions have consequences for yourself and others. There will always come a time in your life when your actions will be judged, and you'll either pay for them or get paid for them.

The meaning of drawing the Justice card depends on the situation and your feelings. For example, if you feel a sense of being wronged, then drawing the Justice card could bring you relief because it could indicate the time for the wrong to be righted. On the flip side, if you have wronged others, then drawing the Justice card could be a warning that your actions will be judged soon.

The reverse Justice keywords are retribution, revenge, lack of accountability, dishonesty, unfairness, corruption, and injustice. If you draw a Justice card in reverse, it could mean many things, including that you are living in denial or running from guilt. These feelings are rooted in past actions, and what you do today will bring about future consequences. You could take the reverse Justice card as an indication to make things right by others so that you have fair outcomes.

In the Fool's journey, the Justice card tells him to take a step back and look at the visions and lessons the Wheel of Fortune and Hermit cards taught him. What do these visions signify for him personally? He also looks back at his life, analyzes the cause and effects of his actions, and, most importantly, takes responsibility for himself. He has evolved as a man. He now knows the art of discernment, based on which he learns to make the right choices. The Fool learns to fight for equality in the form of the world's collective balance.

In Kabbalah, the Justice card is the path between Gevurah and Chesed, wherein Mercy tempers down severity through the hand of justice.

The Hanged Man

The Hanged Man is aware that his position is that of sacrifice. This sacrifice has to be made to move forward. It can be in the form of repenting for past mistakes. The sacrifice can be in the form of giving up certain things to become lighter than before, and moving forward becomes easy. Or it could be taking a step back, sacrificing some progress made earlier so that moving forward happens in a better way through recalculation and recalibration.

The hanged man.
https://pixabay.com/es/illustrations/hombre-ahorcado-tarot-tarjeta-magia-6016939/

The time lost in this act of taking a step back is not lost, but it is used to better understand his path so that the forward movement is significant and outcomes are more accurate than before. The Hanged Man is depicted as hanging upside down to symbolize the spiritual path that he is undertaking. Hanging upside down allows you to get a new perspective, something that people who are walking straight cannot see. This new perspective can lead to spiritual upliftment. The Hanged Man signifies this aspect of spirituality.

The Hanged Man also indicates a period of suspending action, especially during times of indecision. So, it is an indication to postpone certain actions until all aspects are understood well, and the actions can be implemented correctly. In fact, stalling action for a while is one of the best ways to ensure you get sufficient time to make critical decisions correctly.

The upright Hanged Man card keywords are uncertainty, lack of perspective and direction, waiting and contemplation period, martyrdom, and sacrifice. If you draw the Hanged Man card, it indicates a time of waiting and suspension. The card could be a suggestion to stall because it is the best thing to do at that point in time for the best results. It is a reminder that taking action is not always the best solution; sometimes, stalling works better.

The keywords for the reverse Hanged Man are avoiding or fear of sacrifice, apathy, disinterest, indifference, stalling, stagnation, and remaining still. If you draw a Hanged Man card in reverse, then it could indicate a time of indecision. It could also mean that you feel you have sacrificed a lot of time without any benefits. You might feel that you have given everything you have towards achieving something but to no avail.

The planet of the Hanged Man is Neptune, the element is water, and the zodiac sign is Pisces. From the perspective of the Fool's journey, the Hanged Man teaches him that life is not easily tamed, regardless of his daunting efforts to move forward in life. The Hanged Man teaches him that encountering losses and failures are imperative lessons of life that he must learn to succeed.

The Hanged Man card makes the Fool feel defeated for having sacrificed everything for nothing, or so it seems to him. That is when he realizes that relinquishing control over his life is the best way forward, and embracing humility, he inches slowly but surely towards wisdom. In Kabbalah, the Hanged Man represents the path between Gevurah and Hod. It is the path of self-sacrifice that leads to resurrection and renewal.

The Death Card

The Death card is depicted by a skeleton wearing armor, riding a white horse, and holding up a black flag. The armor signifies that death is invincible and no one can defeat it. The horse he is riding on is white to signify purity. Death purifies all. The place beneath the death rider is strewn with corpses from all classes of society – from a beggar to a king – symbolizing that everyone becomes equal in the eyes of death.

The Death card is one of the most misunderstood tarot cards. It is feared without reason, and this is because most people take the Death card to signify death literally. In reality, this card could indicate one of the most positive times in your life. The Death card indicates the end of an old phase and the beginning of a new phase. It means it is time to close the door of one event in your life so you can open the door to another. It is time to put the past behind you and move toward future prospects.

Death.

The Death card could also indicate a change or transition in your life. An old version of "you" has to die to give birth to a new version of you. It is not easy to do this, so feelings of fear are bound to arise. The uncertainty associated with changes can also bring fear. However, once you accept and embrace the changes, you'll see that all has happened for the better.

The keywords associated with the upright Death card are: endings/transformations and transitions/letting go/release. If you draw a Death card, it could indicate a time for transformation. It could indicate that you must be prepared to let go of old stuff, especially unhealthy attachments. The card tells you that holding on to decay and stagnation will only cause harm.

The reverse Death card is associated with fear of and resistance to change, negative patterns repeating in your life, decay, and stagnancy. If you draw a reverse Death card, it could indicate that you have been resisting changes. It could mean that you are scared of letting go of stuff and people. It is a reminder that clinging to things will limit your growth and development. A reverse Death card tells you to relook at your approach to your life or to a particularly nagging problem.

The Death card is associated with Scorpio, the element water, and the planet Pluto. In the Fool's journey, the Death card indicates loss and pain, which teaches him wisdom. He learns to let go of old, limiting habits and embrace new ones to improve his life. He learns to give up the frivolities and non-essential aspects of life. He learns to deal with endings and how to leave the remnants behind. He learns that "death" is a vital aspect of growth. He learns that everyone can rise from death towards newness and growth.

In Kabbalah, the Death card is the path between Tiferet and Netzach. It is the path wherein the lower energy of manifestation leads into the matter of the tangible world. Moving upward involves leaving behind the desire for Netzach (or Victory) and moving towards spiritual beauty.

The Temperance Card

A unisex angel with wings depicts the Temperance card. The unisex aspect signifies the merging or balancing of the opposites. The angel has one foot on earth (the physical world) and the other in water (the subconscious mind). The angel is also holding two cups which can be interpreted as her power to combine the waters of the conscious and subconscious minds into one infinite, seamless flow. This card is a representation of the union of dualities.

Temperance.

The keywords for an upright Temperance card are moderation, peace, balance, calm, harmony, middle path, and tranquility. Drawing an upright Temperance card means you have the wherewithal to remain calm even during stressful times. You are a master of tranquility and will not let any ruffle your feathers.

It indicates that you need a lot of patience to achieve your goals. It suggests balance and moderation for success. The Temperance card tells you to avoid all kinds of extremes and to remain balanced and calm. It indicates that you know what you want and how you want to achieve it. It also indicates that you are at peace with your life and everything happening there. Your ability to adapt is excellent, which empowers you to follow and achieve your dreams.

The keywords for a reverse Temperance card are excesses, imbalance, discord, haste, and recklessness. If you draw a reverse Temperance card, it could indicate some kind of imbalance in your life, resulting in anxiety and worry. When read with the other cards in the spread, you can even determine which aspects of your life are imbalanced. Drawing a reverse Temperance card could also be a warning that a certain path could lead to excesses and discord.

Another meaning of a reverse Temperance card is that you lack a long-term goal or vision in your life, which, in turn, gives no purpose to your life. Therefore, you could feel lopsided. It indicates that you need to step back and relook at your choices before moving forward.

The Temperance card is associated with Sagittarius, the fire element, and Jupiter. From the point of view of the Fool's journey, the Temperance card is a balancing point after swinging wildly since he discovered the Hermit card – until the loss and pain of the Death card. With the Temperance card, the Fool finds true peace and equilibrium, especially after experiencing the storms of the extremes. With the Temperance card, he has combined and balanced all aspects of his life and his personality to achieve wholesomeness. He feels secure and wise. In Kabbalah, the Temperance card is the path between Tiferet and Yesod.

The Devil

In the tarot deck, the Devil is depicted as half-goat, half-man with bat wings. An inverted pentagram is inscribed on his forehead. He appears to dominate and control a nude man and woman lying chained to a stone at his feet, signifying his control over human beings through sensual and materialistic pleasures. The flame on the man's tail and the bowl of grapes on the woman's tail signify their materialistic desires.

The devil.

The man and woman have horns growing out of their head which signifies their connection to evil and devilish instincts as they spend a lot of time in the devil's company. However, despite having their materialistic desires satisfied by the devil, the man and woman are unhappy. Their nakedness is a matter of shame for them as their individual powers have been wrested from them by the devil.

The keywords for an upright Devil card are limitations, excesses, oppression, powerlessness, and dependency. If you draw a Devil card, it means you feel trapped. You are feeling empty and have no fulfillment in your life. It also could indicate that you are a slave to materialistic pleasures and desires. You don't know how to get rid of your excessive love for luxury and opulence eating into your true happiness.

The Devil card indicates that your materialistic greed is taking you into a bottomless rabbit hole, yet you don't know how to break free from the shackles. You seem to be losing control over your life. Substance addictions and abuse could also indicate such feelings of being trapped.

The keywords for a reversed Devil card are freedom, revelation, reclaiming control and power, and release. Drawing a reversed Devil card could indicate a time of self-awareness and a break from shackles. You might be tired of being trapped, and a little spark may have triggered the urge to break free.

While breaking free and releasing yourself from unwanted attachments is great, you must remember that it will not be easy. You must be prepared to make adjustments to break free and learn to be on your own instead of being dependent on things and people that might have given you some comfort even if they also gave you the feeling of being trapped. It is a time for self-assessment wherein you learn what works for you and what doesn't and how to handle what doesn't work for you.

In the Fool's journey, when he encounters the devil, he realizes he is encountering his own helplessness and ignorance. The Devil card reminds him that learning and growing is a relentless part of his journey, and sitting back on the assumption that he knows and has everything will prove fatal.

The Fool also learns that satisfying his material cravings is not enough for his happiness. His search for fulfillment continues, and he realizes that there is something far greater and more important than materialism and physical pleasures and joys. The Fool realizes how deeply bonded he is to materialism and that it is not easy to break free. His wisdom improves as he embraces the idea of overcoming the temptation to pursue his spiritual path. The Devil card is ruled by Saturn, the zodiac sign Capricorn. In Kabbalah, the Devil card is the path between Tiferet and Hod.

The Tower

The Tower card is depicted by a high tower located at the peak of a mountain. The tower has been struck by lightning and is on fire. Tongues of flame emanate from the windows, and people are desperate to escape from the tower. The tower's destruction is inevitable for a new, better tower to come up in its place.

You can compare the significance of these desperate jumping out of the inferno to the desperation of the two nude people chained to a stone at the foot of the Devil card. These people, too, want to escape life's trauma and turmoil. They want to escape the destruction caused by their greed and egoistic arrogance. The Tower card signifies that old ways must be cleared out to welcome something new.

The tower.

The keywords for an upright Tower card are chaos, trauma, sudden changes, and disaster. Drawing an upright Tower card could indicate a momentous change and/or revelation in your life, which could turn your life upside down. However, it need not be something frightening or scary. The Tower card's core message could indicate a groundbreaking change for a much better life than before.

The Tower card sighting need not mean something terrible or painful. It is just a change, a sudden change, but something that is bound to end in a good way. The Tower card fills you with fear because it reminds you to give up some truths you had held dear until now, which is a scary prospect, at least in the beginning. Giving up old ways that you are used to and feel comfortable with takes time and effort, and that fills you with fear and uncertainty. The Tower card indicates that the old ways of your world are not useful to you anymore, and it is time to abandon them.

The keywords for a reversed Tower card are putting off the inevitable, resisting change, and avoiding disaster. If you draw a reversed Tower card, then it could indicate a big crisis looming ahead. More importantly, it indicates that you are struggling to come to terms with it. You don't like the prospect of encountering these changes. The Tower card warns you not to resist what is happening because the good things are at the end of transformations. It is a sign that you must let go of limiting beliefs that have held you back and find your inner strength to become a more authentic self than before.

From the point of view of the Fool's journey, he has realized he is in the Devil's grip. The Tower card is now telling him that only sudden changes can help him loosen himself from the tight clasp of the Devil. He has learned that the devil's fortress is now nothing more than a prison and that he must break down the walls to escape it. A severe shakeup is an essential element for this, the Fool realizes. The Tower's fire blasts ignorance, and he is reborn without the devil's shackles.

The Tower card is connected with Mars, the god of war, the fire element, and Aries and Scorpio. According to Kabbalah, the Tower card is the path between Netzach and Hod, from victory to individualism and intellect.

The Star

The Star card depicts a woman kneeling at the pond's edge, holding two containers. She is pouring water from the pond onto the dry land, which is lush and green, signifying the birth of new life, thanks to the woman's efforts at nurturing and caring.

One of the lady's feet is in the water, signifying her spirituality and mental and emotional strength. The other foot is on dry land representing her physical and practical abilities and strength. Behind the lady are seven small stars representing the seven chakras, or the energy centers in the human body.

The star.

The keywords for an upright Star card are faith, hope, renewal, rejuvenation, and healing. If you draw an upright Star card, then it is an indication of hope and renewal. You'll realize that you are blessed abundantly. It is a reminder that you have everything needed within you to make things happen and to lead a fulfilling, happy life. The card reminds you to have faith because the universe is poised to fulfill your dreams and desires.

Also, if you draw an upright Star card, then it means you have passed a really big challenge. You have overcome this challenge without losing hope. The card tells you you are far more courageous and capable than you think. The card reminds you that you have discovered your resilience.

The keywords for a reversed Star card are negativity, despair, despondence, and lack of faith. If you draw a reversed Star card, you could feel that everything and everyone is working against you. The challenges you face seem insurmountable. You may have lost faith in yourself and the world around you. The reverse card is telling you not to lose faith. Instead, it asks you to dig deep within yourself and find hope to overcome the challenges.

In the Fool's journey, he is coming to terms with the falling Tower. As he picks up the pieces, he turns towards the goodwill he has earned until now and the blessings of the universe to heal and recover.

After the downfall of the Tower, the Fool is filled with serenity, and the Star card reflects this sense of peace he finds. The naked woman on the Star card signifies one whose soul is no longer hidden. The stars above are like a beacon of hope. This fills the Fool with enough trust to counter and replace all the negative energies of the Devil card. His faith is restored, both in himself and the world.

In Kabbalah, the Star card represents the path between Netzach and Yesod, from victory to intuition and dreams. The Star card is associated with Aquarius, the air element, and the planet Uranus.

The Moon

The Moon card depicts a path that leads one to the far horizon. The path is flanked by a dog on one side (representing our tamed, civilized, domesticated nature) and a wolf on the other side (representing our wild, untamed nature). Crawfish emerge from the pond in the card. Two towers on the horizon signify the dualities of life. Interestingly, the similarities of the towers symbolize the difficulty we have in discerning between good and evil. The path that leads into the far horizon is a fine line that separates the conscious and unconscious.

The moon.
https://pixabay.com/es/illustrations/cartas-de-tarot-tarot-luna-magia-6103698/

The keywords for an upright Moon card are intuition, illusion, uncertainty, secretive, complexities, and the unconscious mind. The Moon card represents the dark, which could be interpreted as you walk on the path, unsure of where it is leading you. There could be dangers lurking in the vicinity. The crawfish represents you. The moonlight brings you clarity and understanding. You must allow your intuition to guide you through the dark path.

Drawing a Moon card is a sign of becoming aware of the situation and surroundings and handling the fears and uncertainties in your mind. The card is a warning not to let your inner turmoil lead you to wrong decisions and choices. It reminds you to let go of deep memories and fears hidden in your subconscious mind.

Another interesting indication if you draw an upright Moon card is the existence of an illusion, some kind of hidden truth that needs to be unraveled before it gets the better of you. Alternatively, it could indicate that what you see is an illusion and all is not as it seems.

The keywords for a reversed Moon card are deception, fear, misunderstanding, anxiety, and clarity. If you draw a reversed Moon card, it could indicate that some dark aspects (like the darker side of the Moon) are present in your life. These dark aspects could be in the form of turmoil, confusion, or sadness. Your uncertainty in dealing with them enhances their effects on your life.

A reversed Moon card is a warning that you must deal with your fears and anxieties and that you could misinterpret messages and/or signals. Another interpretation when you draw a reversed Moon card is that all the negative energies are fading away, and you can see the light at the end of the tunnel.

In the journey of the Fool, the Moon card represents vulnerability. Until the previous card, the Fool had learned well from the lessons that life taught him, and now he was calm and serene. This sense of calm itself causes his vulnerability and makes his vision illusionary under the light of the Moon. The Moon card makes the Fool dreamy, making him susceptible to fantasy and distortion of the truth.

The Moon card is associated with the Moon, the zodiac sign Aquarius, and the water element. In Kabbalah, the Moon card is the path between Netzach and Malchut, between love, connection, victory, and the physical, materialistic world.

The Sun

The Sun card depicts dawn, the rays of hope and sunlight that follow the night's darkest hour. It represents fulfillment and optimism. When you see the sunrise, you feel a sense of hope filling your body and mind. The Sun card signifies the same feelings. A naked child playing joyfully represents the innocence that comes when we are aligned with our authentic selves when we have nothing to hide. The child is riding a white horse, which signifies purity, nobility, and strength.

The sun.

https://pixabay.com/es/illustrations/cartas-de-tarot-tarot-sol-magia-6103700/

The keywords for the upright Sun card are vitality, confidence, success, truth, happiness, celebration, and optimism. You will

likely get abundance and success if you draw an upright Sun card. The card renders vitality and happiness to you. You can expect joy and happiness to come into your life.

It also indicates you are feeling fulfilled, which, in turn, makes you inspire others to work towards their fulfillment. Your joy attracts people to you, and you happily spread your energy to one and all. You radiate love to everyone who comes in contact with you. If you draw a Sun card, it indicates that you are feeling highly confident in yourself and your achievements. Life is good as the sun's radiating light shines upon you.

The keywords for a reversed Sun card are over-enthusiasm, unrealistic expectations, pessimism, negativity, pride, and blocked happiness. If you draw a reversed Sun card, then it could mean a time of sadness. It need not necessarily stem from sad events but from the fact that you find it difficult to see the happiness in your life. You are prevented from feeling confident of your achievements, even if your goals are substantial. Certain setbacks could impact your confidence.

A reversed Sun card could also indicate that you have unrealistic expectations; therefore, fulfillment and happiness evade you. Having an overly optimistic view of things could result in disappointment, and a reversed Sun card indicates that. It is a reminder for you to be realistic about things.

The Sun card is associated with the Sun, the fire element, and the zodiac sign, Leo. In the Fool's journey, this card represents that part of his journey cloaked in happy experiences and wisdom. He learned the importance of living and enjoying every moment of his life, and he is grateful to the cosmos for everything.

He realizes that the power and light of the Sun dispel darkness from every nook and corner of his being. Confusions are cleared, and he feels enlightened. He is enthusiastic and filled with vitality and vibrant energy. He is riding on a white horse, eagerly looking forward to a new day and the experiences it will bring.

In Kabbalah, the Sun card connects Hod with Yesod and Splendor with Foundation. This path is an activating force of one's personality as you feel splendorous and yet feel grounded and stable. It is the path of the intellect.

The Judgment Card

The Judgment card depicts Judgment Day as described in various religions. The card shows men, women, and children awaiting their judgment as they rise from their graves in answer to Gabriel's call. Their hands are outstretched, indicating the people are ready to take whatever judgment is given to them. This card reflects the fact that the consequences of your actions cannot be escaped. Judgment will come one day or another.

Judgment.

The upright Judgment card keywords are reckoning, purpose, reflection, self-evaluation, and awakening. If you draw an upright Judgment card, it indicates a time of self-reflection and self-evaluation, both of which are essential to better understand what is happening in your life and your responses and reactions to them.

It indicates that only when you understand your *now*, can you move more confidently into your future, choosing the right path. With self-reflection comes understanding, and with understanding comes the need to make changes and adjustments so that your life path is reset accurately to where you want it to go. These changes and adjustments could be small ones that affect only you or big ones that impact your loved ones too.

When you draw an upright Judgment card, it is a reminder that all are bound to face difficult choices that could have lasting impacts on their lives and those of their loved ones. It reminds you that actions have set your life on an entirely new and unexpected path, and this is the time to face this truth. The card tells you it is time to let go of the past and move on with renewed hope and confidence because every end is a new beginning.

The reversed Judgment card keywords are low self-awareness, self-doubt, and self-loathing. If you draw a reversed Judgment card, it could mean you judge yourself harshly, creating a hazy vision for yourself. For some reason, you hate yourself. In such situations, you are so caught up judging yourself that you miss out on opportunities that have been as clear as day to everyone else but you. It indicates that you are likely to have a period of slow momentum.

Another meaning of drawing a reversed Judgment card is that you must take time out for self-reflection. You must take time out to see how your life is turning out and evaluate the events and happenings. It is time to ask yourself if you are learning life lessons well. The reverse card could be telling you that you have been judging yourself too harshly for your own good. It tells you to forgive yourself for your past actions, let them go, and move on.

The Judgment is ruled by Pluto, the god of the underworld, the fire element, and the zodiac sign Scorpio. In the Fool's journey, he has almost reached the end. This card indicates that he must stop and test his own integrity. The card gives him moral and ethical takeaways from his entire journey.

Here, the Fool is reborn after shedding his false ego and arrogance. His true self is revealed to him, and he realizes that not fear but joy is the core of human life. He forgives himself and feels absolved, knowing and accepting that his core self is pure and sinless. The Judgment card reminds him that his day of reckoning has come, and he needs to embrace the judgments and move into a new future.

In Kabbalah, the Judgment card is the path between Hod and Malchut, between individualism, intellect, and the material, physical world. It is the path that connects your individualism with the physical external world so that you can find an identity for yourself.

The World Card

The World card is depicted with a figure dancing in the center, holding a wand in each hand and one leg crossed over the other. The female figure symbolizes balance and evolution. She also represents fulfillment and completion. However, these two are not static forms but dynamic ones that keep changing and evolving eternally.

The world.

The green wreath around the lady represents success, while the red ribbon around the wreath signifies infinity and eternity. The four figures at the four corners of the World card represent four zodiac signs, namely Taurus, Leo, Scorpio, and Aquarius. They also represent the four evangelicals and the four elements. Therefore, the World card represents the harmonious balance between all the energies of the world.

The keywords for the upright World card are a sense of belonging, fulfillment, completion, and wholesomeness. You can expect fulfillment and completion if you draw an upright World card from your tarot deck. It symbolizes a time when your outer and inner worlds are in sync with each other, and you feel whole and complete.

The card tells you that all your efforts are being fructified and your rewards are starting to come in. It also indicates the completion of a major milestone in your life. It tells you you should be proud of achieving this milestone because you had to overcome many challenges.

An upright World card could indicate that you have successfully completed a long-term project or life event. It could mean marriage, the birth of a child, completing your graduation, or even a big project at the workplace. The World card also indicates that you want to give back to society in some way or another. You are committed to making this world a better place.

The keywords for the reversed World card are a sense of incompletion, lack of closure and achievement, and a sense of emptiness. A reversed World card indicates that you are at the end of some achievement but filled with a sense of emptiness. You feel that all the pieces are not coming together as you envisaged them. You feel some pieces are missing or are in the wrong place. Something is preventing you from feeling accomplished.

The World card is governed by Saturn, the earth element, and three zodiac signs, including Taurus, Capricorn, and Virgo. In Kabbalah, the World card is the path between Yesod and Malchut, between dreams and intuition and the material, physical world. It connects your dreams to practicality.

In this last card of his journey, the Fool learns to take a step back, evaluate, feel the sense of accomplishment of completing the journey, and then prepare himself for the next venture or adventure. He knows that his cycle is complete, the future is full of promise, and he is ready to take the plunge again.

Therefore, the Fool's journey was fulfilling, and his perseverance and hard work paid off. He is not a naive person anymore. He has learned wisdom, picked up knowledge and important life lessons, and has evolved a lot since the start of his journey.

Chapter 7: Meet the Cards II: Four Suites

The 22 Major Arcana cards deal with the larger aspects of your life, while the 56 Minor Arcana cards guide you through your daily, routine trials and tribulations of life. Do not be mistaken by the word "minor" because the impacts of these cards are anything but that.

The cards in the Minor Arcana offer significant insights into your present situation and how you can change or improve your actions for better outcomes. The energies of the Minor Arcana cards in your life are temporary. These energy dynamics change or move depending on your actions and their immediate consequences.

The Minor Arcana is divided into four suites, namely:

• The Suit of Cups

The Suit of Pentacles The Suit of Swords The Suit of Wands Each of the four suites has the following cards:

• Number cards from 1 (or Ace) to 10

• Court cards consisting of the Page, Knight, Queen, and King

The Suit of Cups

The Suit of Cups represents your intuition, emotions, and creativity. In Jungian terms, the Suit of Cups refers to our emotional responses and reactions to stimuli. This suit deals with your relationships and partnerships. It gives you insights into your emotions, emotional dealings, and interactions with others. The Suit of Cups is associated with the water element, fluid and agile.

Ace of Cups - The keywords for Ace (or One) of Cups are new beginnings, fertility and pregnancy, and celebrations. If you draw an upright Ace of Cups, it indicates new beginnings in romantic relationships and partnerships. It indicates a time of joy, empathy, and compassion. Good news could be on the way to you.

If you draw a reversed Ace of Cups, it could be a harbinger of sadness. It also indicates repressed emotions and pain of some kind. You could receive sad, upsetting news. Relationships may not be in the best state of your life. In Kabbalah, Aces or Number one is associated with Keter, the Crown.

Two of Cups - This card is very positive, and if you draw it, it means your life is joyous and happy. Keywords for an upright Two of Cups are mutual attraction and unified romantic relationships and friendships. It also signifies unity in romantic relationships, respect, and affection in partnerships and friendships. If you see Two of Cups in a spread, it could indicate harmony and balance. Reversed Two indicates disharmony, imbalance, argument, and breakups. Number Two is associated with Chochmah or wisdom.

Three of Cups - An upright Three of Cups signifies collaborations, friendship, and celebrations. In the reverse, it signifies independence and "me-time." If you draw an upright Three of Cups, it could mean that someone from your past life is coming back into your life. It signifies groups of people coming together, such as at parties and celebrations. Celebrations and parties could get canceled if you draw a reversed Three of Cups.

Four of Cups - An upright Four of Cups signifies contemplation, meditation, and revaluation. In the reverse, the keywords are withdrawal, introspection, and retreating. Suppose you draw an upright Four of Cups. In that case, it could indicate missed opportunities leading to regret and contemplation on what went wrong. When you see this card in your spread, it is a message for you not to miss out on the opportunities and to grab them. In reverse, the Four of Cups could mean a reversal of bad things. You may have felt stuck in a rut, and this card indicates the difficult time is coming to an end. Four is associated with Chesed, or Mercy, in Kabbalah.

Five of Cups - An upright Five of Cups' keywords are pessimism, failure, regret, and disappointment. A reversed Five of Cups' keywords are self-forgiveness, moving on, and personal setbacks. The Five of Cups indicates a lot of negative emotions, whether you see an upright or reversed card. When you draw a Five of Cups, it means you are focusing on the negative aspects of your life a lot more than needed. An unwelcome sadness is impending in your life. Or you could feel isolated and lonely.

If you draw a reverse Five of Cups, the card tells you it is time to forgive yourself, learn your lessons, and move on. There is no use moping about the past. If you are really struggling with depression, then it might make sense to use the services of a professional therapist. Five is associated with Gevurah or severity, which is aligned with sadness and disappointment.

Six of Cups - An upright Six of Cups signifies childhood memories, visiting the past, and innocent joyfulness. It represents nostalgia. If you draw an upright Six of Cups, it could mean that your past influences you. A reversed Six of Cups signifies living in the past, being overly serious, and forgiveness. Drawing a reversed Six of Cups could mean you are ready to move on, leave home, or start fresh. Six, in the Tree of Life, stands for Tiferet or beauty.

Seven of Cups - An upright Seven of Cups represents choices, opportunities, illusions, and wishful thinking. Drawing an upright Seven of Cups means you have multiple possibilities ahead of you. But it could also mean you are living in a fantasy and indulging in wishful thinking. A reversed card could indicate being overwhelmed by many choices and alignment with your personal choices. A reversed drawing could also mean that you are getting clarity after living in a world of wishful thinking for a while. Number seven is associated with Netzach.

Eight of Cups - An upright Eight of Cups could be abandonment, escapism, withdrawal, and disappointment. A reversed Eight of Cups could mean aimlessly drifting along, indecisiveness, walking away from people and situations, and the desire to try one more time before giving up. Number Eight is associated with Hod.

Nine of Cups - Nine of Cups signifies satisfaction, contentment, and gratitude. If you pick an upright Nine of Cups, your wishes and dreams will likely come true. A reversed Nine of Cups means you find inner happiness and materialistic pleasures. It could also indicate indulgence and dissatisfaction. A reversed Nine of Cups is usually seen as a bad omen where there are fears that your dreams will come crashing down. Number Nine is associated with Yesod.

Ten of Cups - An upright Ten of Cups keywords' are harmony, alignment, blissful relationships, and divine love. A reversed Ten of Cups indicates misaligned values and principles, disconnection with people, and struggling relationships. In general, a Ten of Cups translates to true happiness and fulfillment. A reversed Ten of Cups is not a great sign and could mean that conflicts and arguments will replace happiness and contentment. Number Ten is associated with Malchut.

The Suit of Pentacles

The Suit of Pentacles deals with finances, wealth, and profession. It gives you insights into your financial wealth and career details. It also deals with your external surroundings and how you deal with and respond to them. For example, the cards drawn from this suit will tell you how you deal with money, health, and career-related issues.

How do you see your job? Is it just a way of earning money, or do you treat it as a service? The Suit of Pentacles cards answers these questions. The Suit of Pentacles, at a deeper level, deals with your self-esteem and ego. It is associated with the earth element.

At a Jungian level, the Suit of Pentacles is associated with your sensory information and experiences. How do you react to the information and stimuli your five senses feel or get? It is an indication of your pleasure and materialistic needs and desires and how you go about achieving them. The negative aspects of this suit involve being overly materialistic, greedy, and clingy.

Ace of Pentacles - In general, an upright Ace of Pentacles indicates prosperity and new beginnings. If you draw an upright Ace of Pentacles, it means any new venture you begin is likely to be successful, or a new venture is in the offing. The keywords of an upright Ace of Pentacles are a new career or financial opportunity and abundance.

In reverse, the Ace of Pentacles indicates a lack of vision, planning, foresight, and lost opportunities. If you draw a reverse Ace of Pentacles, it could mean you are not doing enough to prevent prospects from falling through the cracks. You lack focus and control. It is a warning to get your act together.

Two of Pentacles - In the upright position, the Two of Pentacles refers to adaptability and prioritization. It means you are trying to balance the ups and downs in your life and have the adaptability and organizing abilities to do so. It also means there is a struggle between your priorities and those of other people in your life, maybe a loved one or a good friend.

In reverse, it indicates disorganization and a need for reprioritization. Drawing a reverse Two of Pentacles could mean you are biting off more than you can chew. It is a warning for you to go back to the drawing board and reprioritize your stuff. Also, it means you need to save or put aside resources for a rainy day.

Three of Pentacles - An upright Three of Pentacles translates to teamwork, collaboration, learning, and apprenticeship. It means you are working hard to learn and collaborate with other people in your life to achieve success on a solid foundation of knowledge. In the reverse, it stands for working in isolation and misalignment. It indicates that you are not learning from your mistakes because you feel overwhelmed.

Four of Pentacles - An upright Four of Pentacles stands for conservatism and traditionalism, saving money for future security, scarcity, and control. It indicates that you are holding on to situations, people, and possessions. You have a problem with letting go and a desire to control yourself in unhealthy, toxic ways.

In the reverse, it means self-aggrandizement through overspending and greed. It could mean you are engaging in reckless behavior leading to potential harm. However, it also means you have stopped trying to control things and have let go.

Five of Pentacles - An upright Five of Pentacles indicates poverty, financial losses, and worry. It indicates a time of hardship and negativity in your life through job loss and unemployment. In the reverse, it stands for restoring faith and spirituality in your life and recovering financial losses. It stands for a time of recovery from your financial struggles. It also means you are willing to let go of toxic people.

Six of Pentacles - An upright Six of Pentacles indicates a sense of sharing, generosity, and charity. If you draw a Six of Pentacles, it could mean you'll receive generous gifts. Also, you feel like sharing your resources generously. In the reverse, it stands for unpaid debts, only giving and not getting anything back, and self-care. It could mean that someone is giving you gifts but with conditions that may or may not harm you.

Seven of Pentacles - In an upright position, the Seven of Pentacles stands for sustainable results and a long-term view. Drawing an upright Seven of Pentacles means that your hard work and perseverance are beginning to pay off. In reverse, it signifies limited success and the lack of a long-term view. It indicates that your hard work is getting you very little reward or success. It could mean that you are not finishing what you started.

Eight of Pentacles - An upright Eight of Pentacles translates to repetitive work, apprenticeship, and skill-building. It indicates a period of hard work and diligent commitment. You are picking up skills that will be of immense use in the future. In the reverse, it signifies laziness and lack of effort. It also indicates misdirected activity. It could also indicate that you are so focused on one area of your life that you are completely neglecting other equally important aspects.

Nine of Pentacles - In an upright position, the Nine of Pentacles stands for self-sufficiency and financial independence. It indicates freedom and stability. You have worked hard and diligently to achieve success. In the reverse, it stands for being overly invested in your work or profession. You lack confidence and stability. It could also mean that you are getting rewards for which you have not worked hard, and these rewards may not last.

Ten of Pentacles - An upright Ten of Pentacles signifies wealth and financial success and family aspects. You find success and happiness in all aspects of your life, especially in the materialistic areas. You feel closely connected with your family. In the reverse, it represents financial losses and wealth and power's dark side. There is instability and insecurity in your life. A reversed Ten of Pentacles is a warning to avoid shady financial and power deals.

The Suit of Swords

The Suit of Swords deals with your actions, thoughts, verbal expressions, and communication in general. It deals with the mental aspects of human life, including the mind and intellect. The cards drawn from this suit give you insights into asserting your power, expressing yourself, communicating your ideas, and making decisions.

Swords are usually double-edged, and the Suit of Swords symbolizes the fine balance you need to maintain between power and intellect for success and happiness. In Jungian terms, the Suit of Swords deals with your cognitive function and how you process information and data in your mind.

Ace of Swords - An upright Ace of Swords signifies new ideas, breakthroughs, and success. Drawing an Ace of Swords indicates you have great mental clarity and focus, allowing you to make correct decisions. In the reverse, it stands for clouded judgment and doubting ideas and thoughts. Drawing a reversed Ace of Swords means you are confused and led by misinformation.

Two of Swords - An upright Two of Swords indicates an impasse. It signifies that you are weighing options and difficult decisions. It also means you are avoiding making difficult decisions. You are at a crossroads, sitting on the fence, unable to decide. In the reverse, the Two of Swords stands for confusion and indecision. There are delays and postponements. Overwhelming fear and worry are preventing you from making the right decision.

Three of Swords - An upright Three of Swords signifies sorrow, heartbreak, grief, and emotional pain. If this card appears in your spread, a period of difficulty and hardship is indicated. In the reverse, it signifies forgiveness, the release of sorrow, and optimism. A reverse Three of Swords represents overcoming sorrow and heartaches.

Four of Swords - An upright Four of Swords indicates rest, relaxation, and recuperation through meditation and contemplation. Drawing this card upright means a period of stress and anxiety that can be overcome through meditative rest and relaxation. This card tells you that your difficulties are not as bad as you think. You just need to relax, and solutions will emerge. In the reverse, it signifies a period of reawakening and rejuvenation. After some solitude and isolation, you are ready to rejoin the world.

Five of Swords - An upright Five of Swords indicates a desire to win at all costs, competitiveness, conflicts, and disagreements. This card is not really a good sign because it indicates defeat and surrender, but more importantly, a self-sabotaging attitude. It also means there is a lot of stress and conflict in your life. In the reverse, it is a good omen because it indicates reconciliation and making amends. It tells you that the time to end conflicts is near.

Six of Swords - An upright Six of Swords represents a rite of passage, the release of burdens, baggage, and transition. If you draw an upright Six of Swords, it means you'll overcome grief and challenges. You can expect your problems to settle down. You'll be relieved of your burdens. It could indicate travel or a journey, even if it is to escape from troubles for a while. In the reverse, it signifies resistance to change and unfinished tasks. It indicates troubling times ahead and a lack of progress. It could also indicate disruptions and interruptions in travel.

Seven of Swords - The keywords for an upright Seven of Swords are deception and betrayal. If you draw this card upright, it generally means you'll encounter trickery and cheating. It signifies mental manipulations and scheming attitudes. It indicates getting away with some wrongdoing. In the reverse, the keywords are turning over a new leaf and becoming conscientious. It means you regret certain past actions and want to make amends.

Eight of Swords - An upright Eight of Swords translates to self-restrictions, negative self-talk, and a sense of being victimized. If you draw this card, it could mean you feel trapped and pushed into a corner. You feel persecuted and cornered. In the reverse, it indicates freedom from persecution and finding solutions to break free from the sense of entrapment.

Nine of Swords - An upright Nine of Swords translates to anxiety, fears, and worries. The card tells you that your fears may not be well-grounded and based on real problems. It just indicates your inner fears, more likely to be baseless than not. It represents stress and negative thinking. In the reverse, it signifies light at the end of a dark tunnel. It is an indication that your stress and fears are ending. You'll learn to cope well.

Ten of Swords - An upright Ten of Swords signifies hurtful endings, loss, and betrayal. It represents ruin and failure. It could indicate that someone in your life is playing a needless martyr filling you with guilt and depression. In the reverse, Ten of Swords stands for things improving, your mindset clearing and getting better, and surviving the worst.

The Suit of Wands

The Suit of Wands depicts your passions and energy levels. Cards from this suit give you insights into your spirituality and life purpose. They also indicate new and innovative ideas. In Jungian terms, the Suit of Wands deals with our intuition and instincts, the mysteries and secrets of our subconscious, and spiritual aspects and abilities. The Suit of Wands is associated with fire, the hot and unpredictable element. In the same way, this suit deals with our passions and creativity, and if not used well, it can destroy, and if used well can create useful, productive stuff for us.

Ace of Wands - An upright Ace of Wands signifies new beginnings and growth potential. It indicates a time for action driven by passion and enthusiasm. It means you feel bold and passionate about trying new stuff. In the reverse, it stands for setbacks and delays. It could herald disappointing and sad news as well.

Two of Wands - An upright Two of Wands stands for progress, decision-making, and future planning. If you draw an upright Two of Wands, it could indicate having to choose between two paths. It could also indicate overseas travel and sudden journeys. In reverse, it stands for lack of planning and fear of change and the unknown. It also means you have restricted options, and travels could get canceled or delayed.

Three of Wands - An upright Three of Wands indicates overseas travel, expansion, and foresight. It signifies adventure, freedom, and travel, especially to foreign lands and romantic holidays. It is a card of self-belief and self-confidence. In the reverse, it means moving back home or returning from travel. It also warns you about a lack of foresight or planning for the future.

Four of Wands - An upright Four of Wands signifies homecoming, celebration, and joy. It signals parties, weddings, and celebratory events. It indicates a time of stability and security and a time for families and communities to come together. In the reverse, it stands for postponement and/or delays in celebratory events, jilted romances, and leaving home. A reverse Four of Wands could indicate self-doubt and low self-esteem.

Five of Wands - An upright Five of Wands indicates disagreement, conflicts, competition, and tensions. It indicates struggles, opposition, aggression, and flaring tempers. You can expect a lack of cooperation and petty arguments. In the reverse, it stands for ending conflicts and arguments and finding common ground for solutions.

Six of Wands - An upright Six of Wands indicates self-confidence, public recognition, and success. It is an advantageous period for you, and you could win awards and accolades. You could obtain a leadership position in your life. In the reverse, Six of Wands represents failures and losses. You may lose out on awards and recognitions.

Seven of Wands - An upright Seven of Wands' keywords are challenge, protection, and perseverance. Drawing this card means you'll stand your ground and fight for what you believe. It also indicates that someone is harassing and attacking you. In the reverse, the Seven of

Wands indicates surrendering your beliefs. It means you are exhausted and worn out. It could indicate a time when you have lost control and power.

Eight of Wands - An upright Eight of Wands indicates fast-paced transitions, movements, and even air travel. It signifies hastiness and rush. It is a card of fast-paced movements, being energetic, and getting carried away. In the reverse, this card stands for slow progress and low energy.

Nine of Wands - An upright Nine of Wands stands for courage, resilience, and a test of faith. If you draw this card, it means you are halfway through your goal, and your energy is totally drained. You want to give up, but this card reminds you of your courage and resilience. It tells you that your faith is being tested and not to give up. In the reverse, Nine of Wands stands for stubbornness and rigidity. It warns of an uncompromising attitude that can only lead to more harm than good.

Ten of Wands - An upright Ten of Wands indicates extra responsibilities and burdens. Something that was good initially has now become a huge burden leading to stress and anxiety. However, the card also tells you that the end is in sight, and soon you'll be relieved of your burdens. In the reverse, Ten of Wands stands for excessive responsibility and carrying a cross that is too heavy to bear. It could also indicate that it is time to let go and free yourself of your burdens.

Now that you are familiar with the Four Suites and their number cards, it is time to move on to the Court cards discussed in the next chapter.

Chapter 8: Meet the Cards III: Court Cards

The court cards consist of the King, Queen, Knight, and Page; although they belong to the Minor Arcana, too, they set themselves apart from the other cards of each suit.

Understanding the Court Cards

The four court cards appear in each of the four suits. The four represent different figures in a royal court, and a tarot reading can symbolize different people impacting your life in different ways.

The King is the traditional monarch and represents control and authority. The King takes charge of a group and uses his various leadership skills, such as diplomacy, courage, sensitivity, magnanimity, power, maturity, and logic, to lead a team.

The Queen is the court's caregiver and nurturer. The drawing of a Queen card could indicate that either you need the love and care that she can give or that someone in your life is offering loving, protective care to you.

The Knight is the young warrior of a royal court who is known to act rashly and violently but often decisively and for the sake of honor. If you draw Knight Cards, then fast-paced action of some kind could be indicated in your life.

The Page is the youngest member and belongs to the lowest hierarchy in the royal court. He is known for his innocence and one with the most potential for growth and development. Drawing a Page card could be an indication of incoming news or messages. Alternatively, it could be a self-revelation. Further, this card represents any young person or child in your life.

In Kabbalah, the King is the father figure associated with Chochmah, who unites with the Queen, the mother figure associated with Binah. The two of them united to produce the Page (in Kabbalah, the Page is the princess) and the Prince (the Knight card). The Knight is associated with Tiferet, and the Page with Malchut.

The Court Cards of Cups

The King of Cups represents diplomacy and sensitivity. This card in the upright position represents kindness and compassion. Drawing this card means finding the right balance between your heart and intellect. In the reverse, the King of Cups indicates an emotionally immature state of mind with a lack of emotional maturity.

The Queen of Cups signifies empathy and love. Drawing an upright Queen of Cups could indicate a woman who will support and care for you. It is also a card that warns you to be mindful of how you treat yourself and others. In reverse, the Queen of Cups stands for lack of trust and feelings of insecurity.

The Knight of Cups stands for honor and romance. This card carries a lot of excitement through invitations to proposals, events, and other big offers. In the reverse, it signifies heartbreak, unrequited love, and deception. If you draw a reverse Knight of Cups, you could have a one-night stand.

The Page of Cups represents innocence and infatuation. The Page of Cups is a messenger bringing happy news and messages in the form of invitations and potentially useful information. In the reverse, this card stands for bad news and broken dreams.

The Court Cards of Wands

The King of Wands signifies leadership and courage. Drawing a King of Wands indicates that you'll have the energy and enthusiasm to accomplish what you have set out to do. You lead the way for others to follow. In the reverse, it represents boorish and bullying behavior. You are setting a bad example for others.

The Queen of Wands stands for creativity and sensuality. Drawing this card could mean you are getting a lot of work done, thanks to your high energy and optimistic nature. You are always on the go. In the reverse, it stands for pessimism and a temperamental attitude. You have taken on more than you can manage and are exhausted.

The Knight of Wands signifies impulsive adventure. If you draw the Knight of Wands, you feel fearless and raring to go. It is an indication that you must put your ideas into action. In the reverse, it indicates delays and setbacks in your venture and less-than-expected progress in whatever you do.

The Page of Wands represents motivation, drive, and enthusiasm. If you draw this card, you'll likely get good news via phone calls or letters shortly. It is a time to think big and take action toward it. In the reverse, the Page of Wands represents bad news and news of setbacks and delays. You could feel unmotivated and uninspired.

The Court Cards of Pentacles

The King of Pentacles stands for generosity and financial stability. If you draw this card, you could feel proud of your achievement and that your hard work and diligence are paying off. You could be reaching the social status you have been dreaming of. In reverse, it could indicate that you are losing control and cannot see the path of your goals clearly.

The Queen of Pentacles stands for thrift and security. If you draw this card, it means prosperity, success, and high financial status. You'll achieve your goals. In the reverse, the Queen of Pentacles stands for poverty and lack of financial stability.

The Knight of Pentacles represents decisiveness and reliability. This card stands for practicality and common sense. It is a card that indicates you'll achieve your dreams through hard work and perseverance. In reverse, it stands for irresponsibility and lack of common sense.

The Page of Pentacles stands for progress and concentration. If you draw this card, you'll likely get good news regarding wealth and money. It is a card that tells you to start the groundwork toward your long-term dreams. In reverse, it could bring bad news regarding money and materialistic matters.

The Court Cards of Swords

The King of Swords signifies maturity and logic. Generally speaking, the King of Swords represents power, authority, and discipline. It deals with ethics and morals, the key elements of a good king. The King of Swords does not like to show any public display of emotion. Drawing this card upright means an environment of structure and order will work well in the current scenario. A reversed King of Swords represents a lack of self-discipline and structure.

The Queen of Swords represents clarity and intelligence. Drawing an upright Queen of Swords could indicate the entry of a wise, old lady offering counsel and protection for you. She is sharp-witted and honest and loves her wards immensely. A reversed Queen of Swords translates to rudeness, malice, and lack of empathy in your life.

The Knight of Swords signifies debate and confrontation. It is also a card of change and tells you that you must jump in and grab the moment. The Knight of Swords is an intellectual, and if this upright card appears in your spread, it means you have a single-minded focus to complete the task at hand. A reversed Knight of Swords means you are missing out on seeing an excellent opportunity because you are out of your depths.

The Page of Swords stands for self-assuredness and invention. The Page of Swords is all about inspiration and planning. If you draw an upright Page of Swords, then it could be an indication to have patience and to think carefully before speaking. In reverse, the Page of Swords indicates a lack of ideas and planning and is defensive and cynical.

With a clear idea of how each card in the tarot decks works and what they signify, it is time to move on and learn how to create spreads and layouts and how to read them accurately.

Chapter 9: Spreads and Layouts

This chapter will teach you the most commonly used tarot spreads (how the cards are laid out for reading).

One-Card Spread

Set the intention and be clear about the answer you seek. Shuffle the deck as you focus on the question. Pull out the card and lay it on the ground, face up. Look at it and see what it is trying to tell you, especially concerning your question. Refer to the meanings of the cards given in the previous chapters of this book for clarity.

Three-Card Spread

When you pull out three cards for this spread, they can have multiple interpretations depending on your search and need. The first, second, and thirds card you draw can indicate the following:

- Past, present, and future
- You, your relationship, your spouse/partner
- The situation, the action that needs to be taken, and the outcome
- You, your current life path, your potential

Again, set the intention clearly, draw out the three cards, place them before you, and interpret their messages and meanings.

The Yes/No Spread

A yes/no spread works differently for different people. Depending on your connection with the cards in your tarot deck, you can choose certain cards to be a yes and certain cards to be a no. For example, if you feel a strong positive connection with the four Aces, you can choose them to signify a Yes to your question. Similarly, you can choose a few cards that could signify a No. Set your intention, ask your question, and pull out cards until you get a Yes or a No card.

The Celtic Cross Spread

The Celtic Cross spread.

The Celtic Cross Spread consists of 10 cards placed in the form of a cross. This spread gives you deep insights into your queries. Set your intent, shuffle the deck well, and start drawing cards and placing them as follows:

- The first card is placed at the center of the cross and deals with the querent or the seeker, their personality, the state of mind, etc.
- The second card is placed across the first card and represents the blocks and obstacles preventing the seeker from getting what they want
- The third card is placed beneath the two center cards and signifies the root or the underlying reason for the blocks and obstacles
- The fourth card is on the left side of the center cards and stands for recent events affecting the question
- The fifth card is put above the center cards and represents the various available possibilities and solutions for the question
- The sixth card is placed to the right of the center cards and gives insights into achieving the desired outcomes
- The above six cards complete the shape of the cross. The next four cards are placed vertically along the right side of the Celtic cross
- The seventh card is the bottommost of the vertical line and gives insights into how the querent sees themselves in a positive or negative light
- The eighth card, placed above the seventh, represents your environment, including family, friends, and others helping you or getting in the way of your goals.
- The ninth card above the eighth stands for your hopes and fears
- The tenth card, which comes right on top of the vertical line, stands for the outcome, which gives you a fairly accurate result when read along with the sixth card

The Tree of Life Spread

The Tree of Life Spread is based on the Kabbalistic Tree of Life form and consists of ten cards corresponding to the ten Sephiroth. Here's a small breakup for your understanding:

Card Numbers 1, 3, and 5 together form a vertical line with 1 at the top and 5 at the bottom. Card Numbers 2, 4, and 6 are aligned respectively with 1, 3, and 5 on their left, and a gap in the middle for card numbers 7, 8, 9, and 10 starting from the bottom. Card 7 is placed slightly below cards 3 and 5, and card number 10 is slightly above cards 1 and 3. The whole form looks like the Kabbalistic Tree of Life. The meanings are as follows:

- **Cards 1 and 2** (aligned horizontally with each other) represent the issue or the query.
- **Cards 3 and 4** represent people or things impacting the issue or query negatively or positively.
- **Cards 5 and 6** represent the querent's feelings and thoughts.
- **Card 7** represents the physical world, including your body, possessions, and other physical and materialistic aspects of your life.
- **Card 8** represents the querent's persona and personality, how the person lives and presents themselves every day.
- **Card 9** represents the advice your heart is giving you.
- **Card 10** signifies the spiritual or moral outcomes and your own growth in these two because of the issue.

The Zodiac Spread

The Zodiac Spread is also known as the 12-House Astrology Spread and requires you to draw out 12 cards and lay them out in a particular way. As usual, set the intention, shuffle the deck, draw out the 12 cards one at a time, and place them as follows:

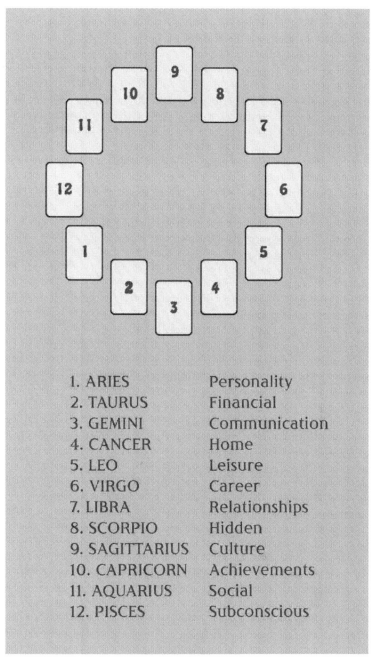

1. ARIES   Personality
2. TAURUS   Financial
3. GEMINI   Communication
4. CANCER   Home
5. LEO   Leisure
6. VIRGO   Career
7. LIBRA   Relationships
8. SCORPIO   Hidden
9. SAGITTARIUS   Culture
10. CAPRICORN   Achievements
11. AQUARIUS   Social
12. PISCES   Subconscious

The Zodiac spread.

Place the first card on the far left of the table. This position is called the 9 o'clock point (as it would look in a wall clock). Then place the other counters in a counter-clockwise direction at every hour of the wall clock.

- **The first card** (at the 9 o'clock position) is your sun sign and signifies your life and personality.
- **The second card** (at the 8 o'clock position) represents your wealth and resources. It is the house of self-worth.
- **The third card** (at the 7 o'clock position) determines your environment, including your family, friends, and people at your workplace.
- **The fourth card** (at the 6 o'clock position) is specifically for your home and family.
- **The fifth card** (at the 5 o'clock position) stands for your creativity.
- **The sixth card** (at the 4 o'clock position) represents your daily routine, including self-care, nutrition, exercise, etc.
- **The seventh card** (at the 3 o'clock position) is about your partnerships, including romantic and other relationships. Even enemies are in a relationship with you!
- **The eighth card** (at the 2 o'clock position) signifies your secrets. It involves taboo subjects such as sex, death, and other topics that one doesn't openly discuss.
- **The ninth card** (at the 1 o'clock position) is about your growth and development, including education, long-distance travel, philosophical growth, etc.
- **The tenth card** (at the 12 o'clock position) is about your profession and career. It is also about how you are fulfilling your dreams and aspirations.
- **The eleventh card** (at the 11 o'clock position) covers your community, including people in your community, social circle, acquaintances, etc. It also deals with charity.
- **The twelfth card** (at the 10 o'clock position) deals with your subconscious mind and reflects your hidden fears and burdens.

Conclusion - Reading the Cards

This last concluding chapter gives insights on how to read the cards in a spread through a few examples. Before that, you must learn a grounding ritual and how to set intentions.

Grounding Ritual and Setting Intention

Before you begin a tarot card reading, do this grounding ritual for stability and protection.

1. Sit down, holding the tarot deck in your hand.
2. Close your eyes and visualize roots growing from your seat that hold you firmly to the ground.
3. Imagine these roots supporting you.
4. Then, imagine an orb of white light covering you entirely, keeping you safe from evil and negativity.

Now, open your eyes and set your intention for the card reading. Here are some tips for setting the intention.

- Write down your intentions. What answers do you seek from the card reading?
- Be clear while forming the intentions. What is your desired final outcome?
- The intention can be in the form of dedication, purpose, prayer, or visualization.

- Repeat your intention while shuffling, drawing the cards, and laying them out in your preferred spread choice.

Interpreting the Cards

When the spread is ready, read the cards using the various astrological, Kabbalistic, numerological, and tarot interpretations mentioned in this book. Here are some examples of reading cards from spreads.

If you have a Six of Swords in the 6 o'clock position (the third card) of a Zodiac spread, then it could indicate a move or travel as this card represents your environment, including daily travel and commute.

Getting an Ace card in the 5 o'clock position (the fifth card drawn) could indicate pregnancy if other factors are in order. Aces are for new beginnings; the fifth card deals with home and family.

Look out for combinations in the spread; for example, in a two-card spread, if you get a combination of an Eight of Wands (that signifies travel) and a Six of Cups (that deals with childhood memories and friends), then it could indicate a journey to meet your childhood friends.

If you are looking for a change in employment and get an Ace in your drawing, it could indicate a new job, as an Ace stands for new beginnings.

Watch out for symbols and images depicted in the cards drawn. For example, if you draw a Judgment and Temperance card in the same spread (remember both these cards have images of archangels), it could mean spirit guides or angels are watching over you.

Suppose you draw cards representing the air element and the water element. In that case, it could mean that you need to balance your heart and head for optimal outcomes.

In this way, you can interpret the meanings of the tarot cards by combining all the knowledge from this book. When you finish reading, remember to thank the divine and close your reading.

Some FAQs

Can I do multiple readings, one after another?

Multiple readings, one after another, can give you confusing, conflicting messages. Stick to one reading that you trust.

Should I rest between meetings?

If you have done one tarot reading and are unsure of the meanings, it is recommended that you wait for at least one more month before seeking answers to the same questions.

What if I'm wrong?

Yes, tarot readings can go wrong for various including but not limited to the following:

- As a tarot card reader, your state of mind could be confused and unclear.
- The tarot querent could be imbued with negative energy that is coming in the way of accurate reading.

In such cases, it makes sense to stop the reading, perform grounding rituals one more time, and then read again. If the problem persists, it is best to put off the reading until you feel ready.

Tarot card reading requires continuous practice and relentless connection with your instincts. Keep practicing until you master the wonderful art of tarot reading.

Here's another book by Mari Silva that you might like

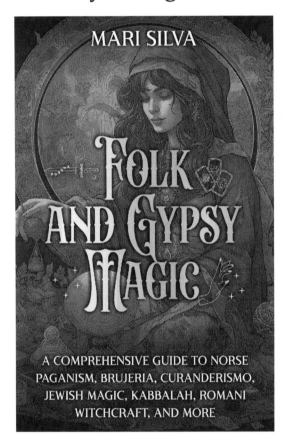

Your Free Gift
(only available for a limited time)

Thanks for getting this book! If you want to learn more about various spirituality topics, then join Mari Silva's community and get a free guided meditation MP3 for awakening your third eye. This guided meditation mp3 is designed to open and strengthen ones third eye so you can experience a higher state of consciousness. Simply visit the link below the image to get started.

https://spiritualityspot.com/meditation

Or, Scan the QR code!

References

A kabbalistic view of the chakras. (2010, April 15). Welcome to the Kabbalah Society. https://www.kabbalahsociety.org/wp/articles/a-kabbalistic-view-of-the-chakras/

ABC News. (2006, January 6). What's behind Hollywood's fascination with kabbalah? ABC News. https://abcnews.go.com/2020/story?id=855125&page=1

Achad, F. (2005). The macrocosm and the microcosm and how by means of the tree of life, we may learn to unite them. Kessinger Publishing.

Archangels - Michael-Gabriel-Raphael - fallen angels - Lucifer-mammo-asmodeus. (2016, November 7). Greeker than the Greeks; greekerthanthegreeks. https://greekerthanthegreeks.com/2016/11/good-versus-evil-eternal-conflict.html

Astrologie proved to be the old doctrine of demons, professed by the worshippers of Saturne, Jupiter, Mars, sunne and moon in which is proved that the planetary and fixed starres are the powers of the ayre, which by Gods permission are directed by Satan ... / written by an unworthy witnesse of the truth of God, John Brayne. (n.d.). Umich.edu. https://quod.lib.umich.edu/e/eebo/A29273.0001.001/1:3?rgn=div1;view=fulltext

Astrology and kabalah. (2015, September 23). Kabbalistic Feminist Astrology. https://kabalicastrology.com/astrology-and-kabalah/

Astrology and Tarot Correspondences: The Minor Arcana pip cards. (2020, July 20). Labyrinthos. https://labyrinthos.co/blogs/learn-Tarot-with-labyrinthos-academy/astrology-and-Tarot-correspondences-the-minor-arcana-pip-cards

Bakula, J. (2017, July 22). Astrology, reincarnation, and the Moon's nodes. Exemplore. https://exemplore.com/astrology/Astrology-and-The-Meaning-of-Moon-Nodes

Belloso, E. (2022, January 27). Mayan astrology 101. Luz Media. https://luzmedia.co/mayan-astrology

Bikos, K. (n.d.). The Jewish or Hebrew leap year. Timeanddate.com. https://www.timeanddate.com/date/jewish-leap-year.html

Celebrity kabbalah: No strings attached, except to the wrist. (2004, July 25). Washington Post (Washington, D.C.: 1974). https://www.washingtonpost.com/archive/lifestyle/2004/07/25/celebrity-kabbalah-no-strings-attached-except-to-the-wrist/18a6a6fc-4a87-4f18-9df8-80478f41b734/

Centre For Psychological Astrology. (n.d.). The centre for psychological astrology - incarnation. Cpalondon.com. https://www.cpalondon.com/incarnation.html

Chatterjee, D. (2020, December 17). THESE are the most masculine and feminine zodiac signs in astrology. PinkVilla. https://www.pinkvilla.com/lifestyle/people/these-are-most-masculine-and-feminine-zodiac-signs-astrology-584543

Concerning the macrocosm and the microcosm and how by means of the tree of life we may learn to unite them, thus accomplishing the great work. (n.d.). Hermetic.com. https://hermetic.com/achad/qbl/qbl-chapter-6

Fernandez, M. (2018, October 1). Reincarnation in astrology charts. Evolutionary Astrology with Maurice Fernandez; Maurice Fernandez. https://mauricefernandez.com/reincarnation-astrology-charts/

Find the sign of your North Node in Astrology: Tables. (2015, April 19). Cafeastrology.com; Cafe Astrology .com. https://cafeastrology.com/northnodetables.html

Fool Tarot meaning, love, feelings, upright & reversed – guide. (2021, March 16). MyPandit. https://www.mypandit.com/Tarot/major-arcana/the-fool

Gemstone for planet Uranus. (2020, July 23). Crystal Meanings & Healing Properties | How to Use Crystals. https://meanings.soulcharmsnyc.com/gemstone-for-planet-uranus/

Gemstones and the 4 Elements - Which one will Work for You? (n.d.). Gemselect.com.

Gemstones and the 5 elements. (n.d.). Gemselect.com

Ginsburg, C. D. (2015). The kabbalah: Its doctrines, development, and literature. Routledge.

Gnostic Tarot kabbalah. (n.d.). GNOSTIC TAROT KABBALAH.

Introduction to calendars. (n.d.). Navy.Mil. https://aa.usno.navy.mil/faq/calendars

Irving, W. (2014). The Alhambra: Extended annotated edition. Jazzybee Verlag.

Kabbalah is an interpretation key, "soul" of the Torah (Hebrew Bible), or the religious mystical system of Judaism claiming an insight into divine nature. (n.d.). New-territories.com.

http://www.new-territories.com/blog/india1/wp-content/uploads/2012/05/kabbalah-sacred-geometry.pdf

Kabbalah, L. (2018, February 17). Nisan – Aries. Live Kabbalah. https://livekabbalah.org/nisan-aries/

Kelly, A. (2018a, February 2). 12 zodiac signs: Dates and personality traits of each star sign. Allure. https://www.allure.com/story/zodiac-sign-personality-traits-dates

Kelly, A. (2018b, October 6). What Houses in your birth chart mean and how to find them. Allure. https://www.allure.com/story/12-astrology-houses-meaning

Kerstein, B. (2018). Kabbalah. World History Encyclopedia. https://www.worldhistory.org/Kabbalah/

Lehrich, C. I. (2003). The language of demons and angels: Cornelius Agrippa's occult philosophy. Brill.

Levi, E. (2019). Dogma and ritual of high magic. Book I. Blurb.

Liselle, R. (n.d.). Which tree is associated with your zodiac sign? | astrology answers. https://www.astrologyanswers.com/article/arbor-astrology-which-tree-is-associated-with-your-zodiac-sign/

Major Arcana Tarot. (2021, April 3). MyPandit. https://www.mypandit.com/Tarot/major-arcana/

Mazurek, D. (2022, November 16). What do the 12 houses mean in astrology? Dictionary.com. https://www.dictionary.com/e/what-do-the-houses-mean-in-astrology/

Media, H. (n.d.). Numerology: Kabbalistic meanings of the number 9. Voxxthepsychic.com. https://voxxthepsychic.com/kabb-numerologynbr9.html

Meijers, L. D., & Tennekes, J. (1982). Spirit and matter in the cosmology of chassidic Judaism. In P. E. de Josselin de Jong & E. Schwimmer (Eds.), Symbolic Anthropology in the Netherlands (Vol. 95, pp. 200–221). Brill.

Planetary Gem Tables. (n.d.). Astrogems.com. https://www.astrogems.com/planetary_gem_table.php

Planets. (n.d.). Llewellyn.com. https://www.llewellyn.com/encyclopedia/article/76

Planets and the sefirot. (n.d.). Librarything.com. https://www.librarything.com/topic/10037

Planets ruling Sephiroth on the tree of Life. (2020, April 14). Enochian Today. https://enochiantoday.wordpress.com/2020/04/14/planets-ruling-sephiroth-on-the-tree-of-life/

Prusty, M. (2018, March 2). 9 planets and their associated gemstones for the betterment of luck. Astroguruonline.com; Manoranjan Prusty. https://astroguruonline.com/9-planets-associated-gemstones/

Sricf, R. N. I. (n.d.). Associations between the royal arch and astrology. Wsimg.com. http://nebula.wsimg.com/9df33fa1cdff047c450b000879cb238f?AccessKeyId=1892C5F96E1E5BB624CD&disposition=0&alloworigin=1

Stardust, L. (2019, December 18). Literally everything you need to know about understanding nodes in your birth chart. Cosmopolitan. https://www.cosmopolitan.com/lifestyle/a30198931/north-south-node-meaning-placement-birth-chart/

Stardust, L. (2022, May 25). Tarot cards by zodiac: See which Tarot cards align with your sun sign. Teen Vogue.

Stelter, G. (2016, October 4). Chakras: A beginner's guide to the 7 chakras. Healthline. https://www.healthline.com/health/fitness-exercise/7-chakras

Sun number in numerology. (n.d.). Astrologyk.com. https://astrologyk.com/numerology/planets/sun

Tarot cards - meaning, sun sign, planet, and element. (n.d.). Probharat.comhttps://www.probharat.com/astrology/Tarot/Tarot-card-meaning.php?card=fool

Teachers, O. (n.d.-a). Astrology. Kabbalah.com. https://www.kabbalah.com/en/articles/astrology/

Teachers, O. (n.d.-b). Meditations for the month of Aries. Kabbalah.com. https://www.kabbalah.com/en/articles/meditations-for-the-month-of-aries/

Teachers, O. (n.d.-c). The kabbalah centre. Kabbalah.com. http://www.kabbalah.com

Teachers, O. (n.d.-d). The kabbalistic calendar. Kabbalah.com. https://www.kabbalah.com/en/articles/kabbalistic-calendar/

The 1st sign of the zodiac Aries. (n.d.). Zodiac Arts. https://zodiacarts.com/elements/astrology/the-1st-sign-of-the-zodiac-aries/

The AstroTwins. (2013, October 19). The 12 houses of the zodiac, defined. Astrostyle: Astrology and Daily, Weekly, Monthly Horoscopes by The AstroTwins; Astrostyle by the AstroTwins. https://astrostyle.com/astrology/12-zodiac-houses/

The letter QOF. (n.d.). ALEFBET - THE HEBREW LETTERS ART GALLERY. https://gabrielelevy.com/pages/the-letter-qof

The letter RESH. (n.d.). ALEFBET - THE HEBREW LETTERS ART GALLERY. https://gabrielelevy.com/pages/the-letter-resh

The seven Traditional Planets. (n.d.). Archangels-and-angels.com. http://www.archangels-and-angels.com/misc/seven_traditional_planets.html

The ultimate flower astrology guide. (n.d.). Flower Actually. https://www.floweractually.com/blogs/news/the-ultimate-flower-astrology-guide

The zodiac Angels – angelarium: The Encyclopedia of Angels. (n.d.). Angelarium: The Encyclopedia of Angels. https://www.angelarium.net/zodiac

Thomas, K. (2021, November 5). A guide to the planets in astrology and what they each represent. New York Post. https://nypost.com/article/astrology-planets-meaning/

Toepel, A. (2005). Planetary demons in early Jewish literature. Journal for the Study of the Pseudepigrapha, 14(3), 231–238. https://doi.org/10.1177/0951820705053850

Yedidah. (2014, July 3). Kabbalah: A language for the revelation of the Divine light. Nehora School Audio. https://nehoraschool.com/kabbalah-a-language-for-the-revelation-of-the-divine-light/

(N.d.-b). Chabad.org. https://www.chabad.org/kabbalah/article_cdo/aid/380211/jewish/Kabbalah-and-the-Calendar.htm

(N.d.-d). Researchgate.net. https://www.researchgate.net/figure/The-Tree-of-Life-or-32-Mystical-Paths-of-Wisdom-linking-the-10-sefirot-with-the-22_fig1_236826988

(N.d.-e). Researchgate.net. https://www.researchgate.net/publication/249768878_Planetary_Demons_in_Early_Jewish_Literature

"12 Astrology Zodiac Signs Dates, Meanings and Compatibility | ZodiacSign.com." Www.zodiacsign.com, www.zodiacsign.com/.

Aliza Kelly Faragher. "12 Zodiac Signs: Personality Traits and Sign Dates." Allure, Allure, 29 Nov. 2018, www.allure.com/story/zodiac-sign-personality-traits-dates.

---. "Am I Psychic? How to Tap into Your Own Psychic Abilities." Allure, Allure, 2 July 2018, www.allure.com/story/am-i-psychic-how-to-tap-into-psychic-abilities.

Alves, Nuno. "The Energy of Spaces and People: How It Works." Energy and Consciousness, 19 Apr. 2015, https://medium.com/energy-and-consciousness/how-energy-works-10893210cc8d

"A Guide to the Planets in Astrology and What They Each Represent." New York Post, 5 Nov. 2021, https://nypost.com/article/astrology-planets-meaning/

Brignac, Wren McMurdo. "What Tarot Cards Represent Which Zodiac Signs? The Story Told by the Major Arcana." Darkdaystarot, 30 Jan. 2022, www.darkdaystarot.com/single-post/what-tarot-cards-represent-which-zodiac-signs-the-story-told-by-the-major-arcana#.

Bunning, Joan. "The Fool's Journey." Www.learntarot.com, www.learntarot.com/journey.htm.

"Chabad.org." @Chabad, 2019, www.chabad.org.

Chanek, Jack. "A Beginner's Guide to Qabalistic Tarot." Llewellyn Worldwide, 9 Dec. 2021, www.llewellyn.com/journal/article/2971.

"Cleansing, Protection & Grounding Methods." Truly Teach Me Tarot, 17 May 2012, https://teachmetarot.com/part-1-minor-arcana/lesson-2/psychic-protection-chakra-cleansing/psychic-protection-supplement/

Coughlin, Sara. "Why You Should Pay Attention to the Court Cards in Your Tarot Deck." Www.refinery29.com, www.refinery29.com/en-us/tarot-court-cards-meaning#slide-4.

CyberAstro.com. "Astrology Benefits in Your Life." Cyberastro, www.cyberastro.com/article/benefits-from-astrology-in-your-life.

David, Lauren. "The 5 Best Tarot Card Decks, according to Professional Tarot Readers." Insider, www.insider.com/guides/hobbies-crafts/best-tarot-cards#the-wild-unknown-tarot-deck-and-guide-set-5.

Deb, Sujata. "Energy Reading Study Guide | How to Read Energy | TheMindFool." TheMindFool - Perfect Medium for Self-Development & Mental Health. Explorer of Lifestyle Choices & Seeker of the Spiritual Journey, 22 Apr. 2020, https://themindfool.com/energy-reading

Ghare, Madhavi. "Structure of a Tarot Card Deck." Tarot-Ically Speaking, 27 Oct. 2010, www.taroticallyspeaking.com/begin/structure-of-a-tarot-card-deck/.

"How to Read a Celtic Cross Tarot Spread." Well+Good, 29 Aug. 2021, www.wellandgood.com/celtic-cross-tarot-spread/.

"Intention-Setting in Tarot Readings (and Everywhere Else)." Practical Magic, www.practicalmagic.co/pm-blog/2021/2/5/intention-setting-in-tarot-readings.

"Introduction to the Tree of Life." Kabbalah Experience, https://kabbalahexperience.com/introduction-to-the-tree-of-life/

"Kabbalah." Glorian, https://glorian.org/learn/topics/kabbalah

Kliegman, Isabel Radow. "Tarot and the Tree of Life." Theosophical Society in America, www.theosophical.org/publications/quest-magazine/1358-tarot-and-the-tree-of-life.

"Learning & Using the Zodiac Tarot Spread." The Simple Tarot, 27 Nov. 2018, https://thesimpletarot.com/learning-using-zodiac-tarot-spread/

Louise, Esther. "Tarot Numerology: Learning the Meanings of Tarot Card Numbers." Through the Phases, 24 Apr. 2020, www.throughthephases.com/tarot-numerology/.

Marina. "Kabbalah and the Tarot - Learn the Connection of Tarot & Kabbalah." City Tarot, 8 Nov. 2018, www.citytarot.com/kabbalah-tarot-minor-arcana/.

---. "The Fool | Tarot Card Meaning." City Tarot, 27 July 2018, www.citytarot.com/tarot-card-meanings-the-fool/.

"Master Number 11 Meaning." Www.numerology.com, www.numerology.com/articles/about-numerology/master-number-11/.

McGarry, Caitlin. "PSA: Your Zodiac Sign Has Its Own Tarot Card." Cosmopolitan, 3 Nov. 2021, www.cosmopolitan.com/lifestyle/a31913908/tarot-cards-zodiac-signs-astrology/.

"Minor Arcana Tarot Card Meanings." Biddy Tarot, www.biddytarot.com/tarot-card-meanings/minor-arcana/.

Parlett, David. "Tarot | Playing Card." Encyclopedia Britannica, 7 Apr. 2009, www.britannica.com/topic/tarot.

"Practical Tree of Life Spread." Mary K. Greer's Tarot Blog, 26 Nov. 2008, https://marykgreer.com/2008/11/25/practical-tree-of-life-spread/

"Tarot.com's Numerology Guide." Tarot.com, www.tarot.com/numerology.

"Tarotscope: How Astrology and the Tarot Are Linked." Two Wander, www.twowander.com/blog/tarotscope-how-astrology-and-tarot-are-linked.

"The Fool Meaning - Major Arcana Tarot Card Meanings." Labyrinthos, https://labyrinthos.co/blogs/tarot-card-meanings-list/the-fool-meaning-major-arcana-tarot-card-meanings

"The Minor Arcana." Thetarotguide, www.thetarotguide.com/minor-arcana.

"The Pros and Cons of Tarot Cards for Mental Health." Healthline, 4 June 2021, www.healthline.com/health/mind-body/tarot-card-can-help-your-mental-health-or-hurt-it#takeaway.

"The Tarot and the Tree of Life Correspondences." Labyrinthos, https://labyrinthos.co/blogs/learn-tarot-with-labyrinthos-academy/the-tarot-and-the-tree-of-life-correspondences

"Thoth Tarot 101: Let This Amazing Deck Guide Your Life." Www.alittlesparkofjoy.com, 16 Sept. 2021, www.alittlesparkofjoy.com/thoth-tarot/.

Wheel of Fortune Tarot Card Meanings. 31 Jan. 2020, https://tarotoak.com/wheel-of-fortune-tarot-card-meaning/

Wigington, Patti. "Where Did Tarot Cards Come From?" Learn Religions, 2018, www.learnreligions.com/a-brief-history-of-tarot-2562770.

Metmuseum.org, 2019, www.metmuseum.org/blogs/in-season/2016/tarot

Made in the USA
Coppell, TX
16 November 2024

40365392R00129